Primary ICT for Teaching Assistants

Also available:
Primary Mathematics for Teaching Assistants
Sylvia Edwards
1–84312–428–9

Primary Science for Teaching Assistants
Rosemary Feasey
1–84312–447–5

ICT for Teaching Assistants
John Galloway
1–84312–203–0

Primary ICT for Teaching Assistants

John Galloway

Routledge

Taylor & Francis Group

LONDON AND NEW YORK

First published 2007
by Routledge
2 Park Square, Milton Park, Abingdon OX14 4RN

Simultaneously published in the USA and Canada
by Routledge
270 Madison Avenue, New York, NY 10016

Routledge is an imprint of the Taylor & Francis Group, an informa business

© 2007 John Galloway

Typeset in by RefineCatch Limited, Bungay, Suffolk
Printed and bound in Great Britain by Bell & Bain Ltd, Glasgow

British Library Cataloguing in Publication Data
A catalogue record for this book is available from the British Library

Library of Congress Cataloging in Publication Data
A catalog record for this book has been applied for.

ISBN10 1–84312–446–7 (pbk)

ISBN13 978–1–84312–446–7 (pbk)

Contents

Acknowledgements

I'd like to thank my family for letting me have a turn on the computer, and being quiet whilst I did, and my extremely knowledgeable and helpful colleagues from the smartest ICT Advisory Team in the country.

Introduction

This book is written for teaching assistants but will prove useful to anyone working with children in primary schools. It begins by taking the strands of the National Curriculum for ICT and shows how these are turned into practical activities in classrooms. Examples are given throughout from across the primary age range so that the educational purpose of this core subject becomes clear.

There are then chapters on using ICT across the curriculum with a particular emphasis on literacy, and numeracy. Finally the spotlight is turned on the role of ICT in inclusion and how technology can make the curriculum more accessible for all learners.

Throughout, this is a practical book that gives guidance on what to do in the classroom in order to help all pupils to learn, whether in ICT as a subject, or using ICT as a tool in other subjects.

John Galloway
May 2006

CHAPTER 1

What do we mean by 'ICT'?

The phrase ICT is unique to education. Other than in schools and colleges people simply talk about IT, information technology. It is in learning that there has been an additional emphasis added, that of the capacity of these machines to both provide information and communicate it. Even then, people in education may still distinguish between IT and ICT, the former being the tools and skills for the job, the latter being what you do with them. So computers, cables, the internet, wireless connections, handheld devices, digital cameras and even mobile phones can be one thing, while word-processing, emailing, video-conferencing and searching on the internet will be the other. Some people also talk of IT as being the skills for using the tools, while ICT is then the use that those skills are put to. Rather like the relationship between using a saw properly and creating a bird table. While these might sometimes be useful distinctions, for the purposes of this book the whole range of equipment and activities will be taken to be part of the one thing: Information and Communication Technology – ICT.

ICT is a very far-reaching and all encompassing term. If we think of the hardware alone that is used in schools it might include:

- computers – desktop, laptop, and handheld, as well as those that just perform one function such as word-processing or data-logging;
- playback and recording – including video machines, video cameras, tape-recorders, digital cameras, DVD and CD players and recorders;
- communications equipment – phones, mobile phones, faxes;
- monitoring – webcams, CCTV, electronic registration;
- everyday equipment – toaster, toys, washing machine, radio, walkie-talkie, microwave, cooker, dishwasher.

Important elements in all of these are: that they are electronic; that we can have some degree of control over their use; that we can choose how they are used; we decide what they are used for; and that they contain micro-processors, some means of processing information.

With such a wide range of resources it is not surprising that ICT can encompass a very wide range of activities, some within the reach of the curriculum subject, some in other areas of the timetable, and beyond. This could include:

- playing at heating a ready meal in the replica microwave in the home-corner of the nursery class, one that hums as its turntable spins and goes 'ping' when the food is ready;
- adding a caption to a digital photo from the class trip to go on display;
- recording a voice-over for a PowerPoint presentation about the principles of hydraulics;
- uploading a poem to the school website;
- emailing the council about the local environment, and attaching photos of the problems, the graffiti, rubbish and broken-down cars;
- calculating the cost of refurbishing the playground on a spreadsheet;
- driving a remote-control car around a circuit;
- programming a car to complete a circuit without your help;
- creating a robot that automatically changes direction when it hits an obstacle;
- videoing the class assembly;
- creating an animation of how the knee-joint works;
- following the travels of a cuddly toy as it jets around the world in a jiffy bag;
- watching a waterhole in Africa, live, as the sun sets;
- video-conferencing with an Egyptologist and asking, 'What does a tomb smell like?'

Many of these activities we might not think of as ICT because these tools are now so embedded in what we do in the classroom that we don't notice the role of the technology anymore. We still, however, need to teach pupils how to specifically use this technology before they can apply it to every aspect of the curriculum. This is why ICT remains a separate subject on the timetable. There are some schools where the skills are taught at the same time as applying them, where asking questions of census information in history is used to teach the skills of filtering, sorting and creating queries in databases. However, the majority of schools seem to have decided that the best model for them is to teach the skills discretely, usually in an ICT suite, before asking pupils to use them in other subjects.

What pupils do in ICT lessons

The kind of activities pupils might do in ICT lessons includes:

- creating and revising text;
- creating and revising graphics;
- combining text and graphics;
- collecting and analysing data;
- performing calculations;
- modelling situations and answering 'what if' questions;
- controlling real and virtual machines;

- combining text, graphics, sound and video;
- creating presentations to communicate ideas;
- finding information;
- communicating electronically.

As you can see, the skills learnt here can all be found in the activities mentioned previously. ICT is the tools, the skills, and their application.

Why we teach ICT is explained in the National Curriculum.

> Information and communication technology (ICT) prepares pupils to participate in a rapidly changing world in which work and other activities are increasingly transformed by access to varied and developing technology. Pupils use ICT tools to find, explore, analyse, exchange and present information responsibly, creatively and with discrimination. They learn how to employ ICT to enable rapid access to ideas and experiences from a wide range of people, communities and cultures. Increased capability in the use of ICT promotes initiative and independent learning, with pupils being able to make informed judgements about when and where to use ICT to best effect, and to consider its implications for home and work both now and in the future.
>
> National Curriculum for England (2000)

What this recognises is that there is almost no aspect of our lives unaffected by new technologies. They affect not only how we work but also how we shop, communicate and entertain ourselves. We are now able to do things with computers that previously took years of training and hours of work: making music; editing films; creating complex artworks. Many tasks previously only done by experts can now be performed by all of us, although perhaps not to the same standard.

That's the what and the why. The how is also important. When using ICT we need to be conscious of our role in modelling the correct way to proceed. This ranges from simple things such as using two hands on the keyboard to more considered ones such as observing proper protocols on the internet (not giving out personal information, for instance).

We also need to equip pupils with the correct vocabulary. The language of a subject is what we use to hang the concepts on that we learn within it. At first this might only mean distinguishing between the 'Delete' key and the 'Backspace' key. As pupils go up the school they will learn about 'Search terms' when using the internet, 'procedures' when programming floor turtles, 'objects' when desktop publishing, and that modelling can be done with spreadsheets as well as on catwalks. Just as with any other subject a good dictionary of ICT terms is a valuable support for pupils – and staff. Pupils should know, for instance, the difference between 'data' and 'information.' The first is facts and figures, the second is those facts and figures given a context and conveying some meaning.

Just as pupils need to learn handwriting to be successful achievers throughout their education and in their lives beyond, they need to become able to use ICT effectively. Like the pencil, the computer (and all associated ICT) is capable of creating an enormous range of work, from subtle drawings to emotionally charged poems or dots on the page of an opera aria. Unlike the pencil, however, this technology may take a lifetime to learn properly, to understand what it does.

CHAPTER 2

What do we teach in ICT?

As we have discussed, ICT is both a subject in its own right and a set of tools for learning in all other subjects. Like literacy and numeracy it provides essential skills that enable learning right across the curriculum. After these skills have been learnt in ICT lessons, they are put into practice in every other area of the timetable, as well as outside of formal lessons, and indeed outside of school.

Like the other subjects in the National Curriculum, ICT breaks down into several strands under two common headings, 'Knowledge, Skills and Understanding', and 'Breadth of Study'. The first of these is what children should learn, the second is the experiences they should have while learning the knowledge, skills and understanding.

There are four aspects to the ICT curriculum:

- Finding things out
- Developing ideas and making things happen
- Exchanging and sharing information
- Reviewing, modifying and evaluating work as it progresses.

These aspects are consistent across the four Key Stages and are developed as appropriate for the age and understanding of the pupils. While it is up to schools how they deliver the aspects, the Qualifications and Curriculum Authority (QCA) has provided an exemplar scheme of work. This provides several themes and lesson plans for each year of primary schooling that, if followed, will cover all the required aspects of ICT. It is not compulsory for schools to follow these, but whatever is taught should be at least as good as the QCA standard, if not better. This scheme of work is available from the DfES standards website: www.standards.dfes.gov.uk/schemes2.

During the years of primary schooling, pupils develop skills by building on the ones they have learnt previously. For example, in Year 1 they might use a bank of words to create sentences, whereas in Year 6 they might be combining words, images, sounds and animations in a multimedia presentation.

Their achievement is measured against the National Curriculum attainment targets. (These suggest that pupils in Year 2 should have reached level 2, and pupils in Year 6 should have reached level 4.) There are, of course, those who achieve higher than such attainment targets and those who do not reach the expected level. There are also those whose attainment is measured against the P scales (so called because they are 'pre' National Curriculum levels).

The rest of this book will look at how you can help pupils achieve in ICT, and also in other subjects when using ICT. It will also consider how you will know what level they have got to, and how we can harness the power of this technology to support the inclusion of all pupils in the curriculum.

Helping children find things out

'Finding things out' in the National Curriculum is just that, researching and dealing with information in various forms. There is an expectation that during Key Stages 1 and 2 pupils will:

- 'gather information from a variety of sources';
- 'talk about what information they need and how they can find and use it';
- 'enter and store information in a variety of forms';
- 'prepare information for development using ICT, including selecting suitable sources, finding information, classifying it and checking it for accuracy';
- 'retrieve information that has been stored';
- 'interpret information, to check it is relevant and reasonable and to think about what might happen if there were any errors or omissions'.

The information referred to is not just that found through electronic, technological means, but any information from many and various sources, as well as the skills necessary to find it. And it's not just the finding of it but also the evaluation of it, for validity, accuracy and reliability. There is also re-formatting it, to use it for different purposes. Knowing that what you've found really is what you want to know, and then thinking about how to present it for other people to understand.

There are a number of aspects to this strand of the ICT National Curriculum. One is the use of sources that are not electronic, realising just how we know what we do from everyday sources. Another is the use of electronic sources such as CD-ROMs and websites and how we use these efficiently. And a third is more formal collection and interrogation of data through records and databases of different types. Finally there is the question of what we do with the information once we have found it, how we interpret it and reproduce it for other people and purposes. All this is underpinned by key vocabulary that builds throughout the scheme of work and critical skills such as evaluating the usefulness and validity of what ever we have found.

We get information from many different sources, some of them fairly obvious and some of them less so. This is why the earliest lessons in this strand focus on what we see and what we hear and what these tell us. We take in a lot of information without realising it. The first step here is to make children aware of what information is and how they discover it.

Starting with sounds and images

MAIN IDEAS

Information comes in a variety of forms from a number of sources, which might be computer based.

USEFUL VOCABULARY

information, text, graphics, sound, button, icon, multimedia

TRANSFERABLE SKILLS

Recognising that we can get information from lots of different sources, including our environment.

Sounds

At the beginning we can focus on what we see and hear, and what we learn from this. We can ask children to identify common sounds and ask them what information they give us. A recorded tape of everyday noises might include:

- the school bell;
- an ice-cream van;
- the theme tune to a children's TV programme;
- the wheel in the hamster's cage;
- a running tap;
- a doorbell;
- a vacuum cleaner;
- the rustle of a crisp packet.

After each sound children should say what it tells us, what information it gives, not just what the sound is. The school bell might tell us break time is over. The squeak of the hamster's wheel tells us it is exercising, and a running tap might mean someone is pouring a drink. So questions to ask might include:

'Why might the tap be running?'
'Who could be at the door?'
'What would your dad use the vacuum cleaner for?'

Symbols

You can do similar activities with images. One of the earliest steps to literacy is to recognise that symbols carry meaning, that is, letters represent sounds that build to make words. Many schools use symbols all around the school to help pupils understand their environment and to guide them through the school day, whether these are for very young children, or those with special needs, or even those for whom English is an additional language. These can range from line drawings to photos showing activities. Children can be very quick to learn their meaning. Very few would not understand what a pair of golden arches in the shape of the letter M mean – although their response might be a bit different to yours.

Visually, children should understand that both signs and symbols, and pictures and photos, tell us things. The former are often representations that give us information, pupils can look at the signs on the toilet doors to know whether they are for boys or girls, even though the image is not a specific representation of either. Some signs may be in particular colours, red for danger perhaps, while others will be written larger, or in a variety of font sizes. Similarly they could look at the school crest or logo and see what information that carries. It may just be initials rather than the school name, a local feature may be included, or an animal from a patron's family crest. Here the information, or the image, may be abstract; when they look at pictures or photos it is likely to be more concrete.

Photos

A photo of a landscape, for instance, might give sufficient information for them to know what season it is, the sort of weather or climate, the time of day, the type of place it is (town, countryside, by the sea) and some clues about what it would be like to live there. When asking the children about what they can tell from the image it is important to get them to think about not just what information they can get from it, but also how they know. It might be late in the day because of the position of the sun in the sky, or maybe because there are long shadows. It could be a hot climate because everyone in the photo is wearing T-shirts. You may also want to get the children to think about what information they cannot get from a particular image. They probably won't be able to tell what people's names are,

Figure 3.1   The wedding of Roger and Brenda Haslam, 31 March 1956 (the author's in-laws)

how they are related to each other, or just when a photo was taken. It may be possible to suggest an era because of what they are wearing, but probably not anything as precise as a year.

We can ask a number of questions about the photo in Figure 3.1 with varying degrees of challenge.

'What is happening here?'

'Why are these people dressed this way?'

'Why are some of them wearing similar clothes?'

'What time of year is it?'

'Was it taken recently or a long time ago?'

It is important for children to understand not only what information can be found from a particular source, but also what can't. This is a theme that continues throughout their studies in ICT: How do you select a suitable source for information, and when you have, how can you tell if it is reliable? A sepia photo may indicate that it is old, or it may be due to the settings used on a modern digital camera. Whenever appropriate the question of reliability and validity should be raised.

Describing and depicting

MAIN IDEAS

We can use key words to describe objects.

Data can be collected and presented in different ways.

USEFUL VOCABULARY

pictogram, graph, classify, sort, key words, tree

TRANSFERABLE SKILLS

Identifying sources of information, asking well-formed questions and checking the validity of answers.

Presenting information in different ways for different audiences.

As a first step to sorting and classifying data, children can be asked to describe the attributes of various things and shown how information can be represented graphically. For a start they could be asked to pretend they have lost something then describe it to the rest of the group without saying its name. It would be helpful here to model this for children first, describing something yourself and asking them to guess what it is. You can move on from here by using logic blocks, asking children to describe 3D shapes by size, colour, sides, and so on.

At this point they will also begin to develop an understanding of the graphical representation of information, that is, that pictograms and graphs can be used to answer questions or show what they have learnt. For example, reading a pictogram of how children travel to school or creating a pictogram of different eye or hair colour in the class.

Using electronic sources

MAIN IDEAS

Electronic sources, such as CD-ROMs and the internet, can be searched in a number of ways to find information. Pupils can then use the information they find to help present their own ideas. Thought needs to be given to issues such as whether the information can be trusted or has a particular bias.

USEFUL VOCABULARY

search, menu, hyperlink, bookmark, URL, search engine, bias

TRANSFERABLE SKILLS

Becoming familiar with the structure of electronic information sources, how to search them, follow links and use buttons, icons, web-page addresses and bookmarks.

Staying safe on the internet.

The first electronic information sources children encounter may well be online dictionaries and encyclopaedias, or either of these on CD-ROM. The internet is becoming more widely used but there is the possibility of becoming overwhelmed by the volume of material there and lost among the innumerable pages of information. With a CD-ROM children can remain within the one source and, if they find they have followed a link they didn't mean to, use the 'Home' button that is usually there to start again. In fact, before allowing children to explore these sources they will need to have some guidance about how they work.

To begin with look at the different icons on the page, discuss what they might mean. There will usually be one with a house on it to take you 'Home', that is the opening page of the CD-ROM. Then there are forward and back buttons, probably a magnifying glass or binoculars to go to a search page, and often a pencil to make notes and a printer to print out the page. It will help pupils to know that while these won't be the same on every CD they use, these functions are likely to be there somewhere.

They will also need to know about 'hot spots', or 'hyperlinks', places in the text and on the images or the buttons where a click will take them to another point in the resource. These will be shown by the cursor changing from an arrow to the browser finger. As they begin to learn to navigate the CD they will be learning some of the skills necessary to use the internet, but they will also be using skills from books, like using chapter headings or looking in an index. As with printed books, the information they want may be in a particular chapter, parrots may be under 'Birds', or maybe 'Rainforest'. Here, though, there will be several ways to get information from the text, and pupils need to be comfortable with all of them.

Searching the internet

Similarly, with the internet, children need to know what the buttons mean, but also how to use tools such as bookmarking (adding a reference to a page to a saved list) and open new pages by using the right-click menu.

The use of the internet to find information is becoming more common, mainly because of the quality and extent of the resources available, and children are using it at a younger age than previously. Whereas the QCA scheme of work introduces it in Year 6, many pupils will have been regular users at home for some years by then. Certainly their use may have been restricted to playing games or following up favourite TV programmes rather than research, but they will be familiar with using addresses, links and buttons.

When first using the internet to find out information it is best to do a search in advance and bookmark the pages you want them to use. To create a bookmark, find the page you want, then follow Favourite>Add to Favourites in Internet Explorer, then choose New Folder and give this a clear name, so you can keep all the links for each topic in an organised way. This way you can contain the amount of information they need to deal with. You may also want to let them print out particular pages and use a highlighter pen to focus on key information, which may prove easier than scrolling up and down and copying it off the page.

As pupils become independent there are a few things they need to know.

How to use a URL

URL is an abbreviation of Uniform Resource Locator. This is the technical name for what we might more commonly call an internet address. These always start with HTTP but you don't need to type this in. HTTP stands for Hypertext transfer protocol, the computer language the internet is written in. It is useful, though, to understand how these addresses work. Most commonly they start with www (for Worldwide web) and their name is chosen by the owner of the site. This could be a public institution, such as the BBC, a company like Lego, or a private individual, such as John Galloway. The next part of the address, the extension, tells you what sort of institution this is. Here is a list of what they mean:

.com – company (.co is the same thing but needs to be followed by a country)
.gov – government
.sch – school
.ac – post-school educational institution such as a university
.org – an organisation such as a charity.

Others include: .biz, .net, .info, .me, and .tv.

The country extensions include:
.uk – United Kingdom
.nz – New Zealand
.au – Australia
.fr – France
and even .pn for the Pitcairn Islands.

From these elements different addresses can be built. For instance, www.canterbury.org.uk will give you information about the City of Canterbury in Kent, but switch the ending to nz and it will give similar information for New Zealand; or change the 'org' to 'ac' and you will find their respective universities. That these minor changes can make a big difference helps explain why sometimes you don't get what you expect from an internet search.

Effective searching

Searching on the internet can lead to some confusion, with more information becoming available than is needed, and some pages contradicting each other. The most popular search engine currently in use is Google at www.google.co.uk, although there are many others, including some especially for children, such as Ask Jeeves at www.ajkids.co.uk. You could also try www.yahooligans.com.

The way a search engine works is to look for pages containing the words entered, the 'search terms'. However, a search engine looks for any page containing the words, and sometimes any page containing any of the words. So a search on the two-word term 'Egyptian Gods' could produce more than 2 million results. However, put speech marks around the words 'Egyptian Gods', and the search engine will only search for pages where both words occur adjacent to each other. This time there are about a quarter of a million, a reduction of 80 per cent. But still too many to flick through easily.

Most search engines provide the most relevant results first, although companies can pay to push themselves up the list, so sometimes retail sites get top billing. It is here that being able to assess the URL can be very useful. The URL www.ancientegypt.co.uk sounds as though it will have the necessary information, whereas www.amazon.co.uk will offer to sell you a book about the subject. You will need to discuss how to assess sites with children so they can judge for themselves which sites from the returned list seem most promising.

Even so, there are times when it is necessary to be very discriminating and discuss with children just what information they have found, as even seemingly reliable sites can give dubious information. A search for 'Darwinism' or 'evolution' can produce results from websites promoting the notion of 'intelligent design', a concept based on religion rather than on science and which refutes Darwin. Pupils need to be taught about perspective, point of view and bias. It is helpful to talk through what results might be expected before searching, and to welcome open discussion of anything that seems unusual.

Copying and copyright

Once they've found the information, getting it off a web page is quite straightforward, which is why there is so much concern about the internet being used for older students to cheat by exchanging essays. Sometimes it is easy to tell whether pupils have copied information simply because of the language used. If you are not so sure, you can check by running a search yourself using some of the key phrases and see what comes up. However, the best way to stop pupils from simply nicking other people's work is to set them tasks that force them to re-process it rather than repeat it, just like when they are working from books. This could take the form of asking them to create a newspaper report from firsthand accounts, or a first person diary from a timeline, tasks that require them to interact with the text.

Having said that, though, there are times when it is very useful simply to be able to copy what is there (perhaps when you are making a worksheet). To copy an image:

- point at the image you want to copy;
- right click and select Copy from the command menu that appears;
- switch to an open application, such as MSWord or PowerPoint;
- click on the page where you want to put the image;
- right click again and choose Paste.

Copying text is much the same, only you need to highlight the writing to be copied from the web page before right clicking. (The only complication is that sometimes web pages use tables in their layout so the table is copied into the other document too. If this happens, simply Select All in the Edit menu then from the Table menu choose Convert Table to Text.)

However, whatever is on the internet will be copyrighted in some way. That is, the person who created it has the right to say how it can be used and to be acknowledged as the originator. Quite often a website or reference work will contain a copyright notice; this should be complied with.

Even then, copyright will seldom be a problem as children copying from web pages for their own work are unlikely to breach it, as long as they are copying only for educational purposes and not re-publishing. However, if children create a website and find a piece of art they like and put it on their own site, without saying where they got it from, they are likely to be in breach of copyright. By putting someone else's work on the internet they are re-publishing. It is always good practice for children doing research to state their sources. They can also link their own pages to those of the originator of any work to ensure that due credit is given.

Keeping children safe on the internet

The majority of the 6 billion plus pages on the internet contain material not designed for children. Much of it is completely unsuitable so you will want to take steps to keep it from them. As mentioned previously, one method is to find the pages you want the pupils to use, create a folder in the Favourites of your web browser for whatever topic you are covering, then bookmark into that folder the pages you want them to use.

As they go up the school you will want to allow pupils more freedom. Fortunately most school systems have 'filtering'. This is an electronic tool that detects unsuitable content and blocks it out. Most filters can be modified so any unsuitable pages that do get through can be reported, or anything that should be allowed can be notified and viewed a little later.

Regardless of how good a system is put in place there are usually ways around it that some pupils may actively try to find. In these instances the school's 'Acceptable Use Policy' should be referred to. Every school has one of these policies, which specify how children will use the internet and what sanctions will be imposed if they breach this. Quite often an acceptance letter for this policy is part of a package sent out for parents to agree to at the start of every school year.

Children should also be taught to monitor the internet themselves and to report any inappropriate pages to an adult, along with learning the skills of thinking about the information they find and its validity, and those of questioning and discrimination.

Other ways to protect pupils when using the internet can found under 'e-safety' on the Becta Schools website (schools.becta.org.uk). These include:

- monitoring the use of email, particularly web-based mail such as Hotmail, perhaps restricting pupils to using class-based addresses;
- restricting the use of chat rooms to educational sites;
- ensuring computer rooms are supervised when pupils are using them;
- and because of the risk of viruses, not allowing pupils to download files from the internet without staff permission.

As a source of information the internet is boundless, like a vast library. And just as a library has rules, so should the use of the net. There should be some supervision of pupils' use, either at the time or by examining the history. They can be guided to particular sources, and be ejected if they break the rules.

Recording data electronically

MAIN IDEAS

We can use electronic sensors to record information about our environment.

USEFUL VOCABULARY

sensor, light, temperature, monitor, measure, reading

TRANSFERABLE SKILLS

Describing things accurately.

Understanding similarities and differences.

Methodically gathering information.

Children will probably be used to using measuring tools such as thermometers and rulers. They need to be aware that we can monitor changes over time by using electronic sensors that can also measure light or sound.

To begin with the children can just be shown how the sensors work. With sound they can see what the reading is if they all sit silently. Even with everyone being quiet there may still be a reading that can lead to discussion about background noise and sensitivity of the instruments. Heat sensors can be used to check the temperature of warm drinks, radiators, window glass or even armpits.

Once the pupils understand how the sensors work they can be applied to a number of tasks. A simple one is to monitor the rates at which liquids cool in different sorts of cup, such as polystyrene, ceramic or paper, to see which has the best insulation. Another might be to monitor sound in the classroom to see which is the noisiest lesson.

Once the data is collected it needs to be analysed in some way to make sense of it. As it is collected over time, line graphs will show what happened. Questions to ask include:

'What are the highest and the lowest measurements? What was happening then?'

'Are there times when there is no change? Why do you think this is?'

'Could we have recorded this data without a computer? If so, how?'

'Are there any advantages to using electronic sensors?'

Handling data electronically

MAIN IDEAS

We can use software to record and query data and we can use databases to do this. We can use different questions to find answers and create graphs, charts and reports. We need to check that the data is reliable.

USEFUL VOCABULARY

sort, classify, database, field, record, file, order, bar chart, pie chart, line graph, bias, AND, OR

TRANSFERABLE SKILLS

Creating records, recording and interrogating data with queries and searches.

Asking useful questions and considering the plausibility of results.

There are two interconnected ways of handling data that children will be introduced to. One is using branching databases, where objects are sorted according to a series of questions (often simply 'yes' or 'no') that focus on unique characteristics. The other is using records of information that can be sorted and queried. There are children's games that are useful to introduce either approach.

Branching databases

'Guess Who' consists of two sets of identical cards in a framework where all the cards are standing up and are then turned down if they meet certain criteria until only one card is remaining. The object is to use questions such as 'Is it a woman?' or 'Do they wear glasses?' to find the unique characteristics of a particular person or object. In a branching database to identify fruit, for instance, we might focus on its colour, shape or flavour. Questions might include:

Is it green?

Is it round?

Is it sour?

Is it a citrus fruit?

The object is to filter out all the options until it can be only one particular thing. If, for instance, the last question is 'Is it yellow?', the answer could be banana or lemon, so another question, such as 'Is it long?', which can be answered with 'yes' or 'no', can be added to separate these two.

The approach displayed in Figure 3.2, a branching database, can be used in some subjects, particularly science, right into secondary school. It is the principle that underlies the creation of keys to identify species.

As with many aspects of ICT, beginning with a concrete experience can help create foundations for understanding. One way to help pupils learn how a branching database works is to play a game with them in which they are uniquely identified, by a set of characteristics that only they match.

Start with the whole group. An easy way to divide them initially might be into boys and girls or above a certain height. Ask more specific questions until only one or a few pupils are left. Later questions could include Brownies or supporters of Charlton Athletic. The idea is to generate questions that separate them and uniquely identify them.

Another approach could be to start with real objects, such as biscuits, and find ways to separate these – sweet, savoury, brown, pink, round, oblong and so on. By using bits of string or strips of paper a structure can be created for pupils to follow to create their own branching database.

As they progress through the school pupils will be able to create branching databases with increasing sophistication. For example, they might want to think about the different materials they could use to build a car or why strength or weight or pliability do not always go together.

When introducing more complex databases, where items can be distinguished or grouped and sorted by more than just a simple 'yes' or 'no', another set of popular games might be useful – the 'Top Trumps' series.

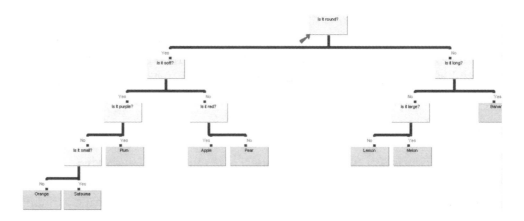

Figure 3.2   A branching database to sort fruits using Decision3

Each playing card is a record card with data fields that players use to overbid their opponents. When starting to introduce databases the use of actual record cards, rather than digital ones on screen, helps to root the processes in a real experience.

The first approach will be familiar. We move from the concrete to the more abstract by taking a range of information sources, such as books, magazines, images and so on, and discuss how it can sometimes be difficult to find what we want. If the information is organised we can find things more easily, we can ask questions of it and we can reorganise it and present it differently.

We can then begin to introduce children to the technical detail of a database, although not electronically just yet. We can talk about 'records' being all the information about one thing, and 'fields' being each piece of data held on it. At this point it is best to use cards with the information on and ask children to read them, add to them, create their own and sort them in different ways. For instance, a set of cards on mini-beasts can be sorted into those with or without wings, they can be ranked by number of legs, or put in order of size. More data can be added by leaving blank fields and asking children to complete them, or giving them blank cards and pictures of creatures to measure and record.

From here the same information can be presented on the computer in a database. The children will already be familiar with the content and will be able to make the link between the cards and the information on screen. It will help to have the cards and point out that the same information appears in both forms. You will want to reinforce the vocabulary of fields and records, demonstrating where they are on screen. The information may be presented a bit differently, in another order, or as a table rather than one record at a time.

When introducing the database you can also discuss the formats the fields take. Some will be choices, 'yes/no', 'male/female', others will be numbers, such as dates or measurements, and some will be text, colour perhaps or a note about locality. Children need to understand that accuracy in inputting the data is important, that if we put letters in number fields, for instance, the computer won't be able to 'sort' the data properly. Although young children will probably be measuring in centimetres you might want to talk about the need to always use the same scale, that we cannot mix centimetres and millimetres, or grammes and kilogrammes.

Interrogating datasets

One of the easiest datasets to use when introducing databases is the children themselves. A new database can be created with one record per child and everyone can be involved in measuring and entering. Records could include the obvious ones such as:

- height
- eye colour
- hair colour
- shoe size

as well as the less obvious such as:

- hand span
- reach from finger tip to finger tip
- length from heel to knee

and survey type questions like:

- favourite food
- favourite cartoon character
- type of pet
- number of siblings.

There are many ways in which this data can be interrogated, however it will help to start by getting the children to 'sort' themselves. Use a large space such as the hall or playground and find ways of grouping and regrouping, of creating 'queries.' Obvious ones are to line up in order of height, or age. Less obvious, is to mark out 12 months on the floor and create a bar graph of month of birth with children lining up behind the marks. While it may seem obvious you will want to point out to them that some months have more birthdays than others and ask questions such as:

'Which month has the most birthdays?'
'Is any month empty?'
'Which has the least?'
'Do any have the same number?'

Subsequently, when you use the same queries on the computer database the children will be able to make a direct link to the activity in the hall. However, you will also be able to ask different ones:

'Which is the most common eye colour?'
'What is the largest number of siblings? And the smallest?'
'How many different forms of transport are used to come to school?'

Some of these can be presented as bar graphs, or pictograms to show how presenting information graphically can make it easier to understand.

As children go up the school so the questions asked and the graphs and charts used can become more complex.

'Do boys have wider hands than girls?'
'Do taller children wear bigger shoes?'
'Are blonde haired children more likely to have blue or brown eyes?'

Some of these can be more usefully presented as line graphs or pie charts. For instance, a graph showing girls' heights on one line and boys' on another will help answer the question of whether one gender is generally taller than the other. A pie chart of blonde children's eye colours will show what the different proportions are.

As children ask more complex questions so they will need to learn how to structure them in order to get answers that are accurate or meaningful. At first they may 'sort' by a particular criteria, such as height, or 'group' by hair colour perhaps, then they will begin to use terms like 'AND' as well as 'OR'.

A query on favourite colours could be run on the fields Gender and Favourite Colour to find out how many boys like green.

'Gender: Male AND Favourite colour: Green.'

We might want to widen the criteria to include blue.

'Gender: Male AND Favourite colour: Green OR Blue.'

Another question might be how many pupils overall like green.

'Gender: Male OR Female AND Favourite colour: Green.'

This approach can be applied in other aspects of the curriculum, in science for instance for distinguishing between creatures, a database of various mammals; or properties of metals.

There will also be times when pupils will be asking questions with certain limits. For instance, in our database about the children we may want to find out how many are above or below a certain height, here we can use the '=<' and '=>' operators. These mean 'equal to or less than', and 'equal to or more than'. To find all the children smaller than 110 centimetres we could ask, 'Height =< 110'; for those above 130 centimetres it would be 'Height => 130'; and to find a range between we can ask 'Height => 110 AND =< 130.'

Some of these approaches, particularly the use of AND and OR can be helpful when refining searches on the internet.

Is the information any good?

MAIN IDEAS

Children need to be able to make judgements about the quality and reliability of the information they find.

USEFUL VOCABULARY

valid, bias, reliability

TRANSFERABLE SKILLS

Finding suitable sources of information, assessing reliability of information, considering viewpoints.

As children progress through primary school the sources of information become more varied and complex. From looking at photos and listening to tapes they will begin to use books, magazines, CD-ROMs, the internet and databases. They will need to consider the advantages and limitations of all of them.

Opportunities to handle information will occur right across the curriculum and these can offer the best chances to address the issue of assessing information.

For instance, when thinking about different places we might want to locate them on a map. A computer screen offers less space than an atlas, so it is harder to see somewhere in relation to the places around it. However, borders change and atlases become out of date, whereas information on the internet can be updated. Websites such as www.maps.google.co.uk are easy to manipulate, the scale can be quickly changed and even overlaid with aerial photos. However, it may be less easy to work out on the internet what countries are on the borders than in a book, or with a ruler or scale. Similarly information about population or industries of other countries might be more easily gathered from a book, but it may not be as up to date as the CIA World Book website (www.cia.gov).

Using American websites or CD-ROMs is a useful way of introducing the idea of discriminating between information. A search for 'football' or 'Birmingham' may very quickly begin to produce pages of information that will seem rather alien. You will want to discuss with children how they can tell which are useful web pages and teach them to use these skills to discriminate and sort.

Now I've found it, what do I do with it?

Finding out information is only part of the task; interpreting or using it is the rest of the activity. Quite often interpreting or using information appears across the curriculum as the skills learnt in the ICT suite are applied in other areas of the timetable. For example, charts and graphs are used in mathematics and science but can also help in subjects such as history. Here, children might use pie charts to show how many people lived in towns or the countryside and how this changed during the Industrial Revolution. They might also use images and information to produce newspaper front pages about historical events.

As stated previously, they will need to respect copyright when using others' information, particularly if their work is made available on the internet. Similarly, they have the right to expect that what they produce will be respected by others. Overall, though, the intention is not just to find information, but to do something with it, so showing it to others, having an audience, is part of the learning experience.

Helping pupils develop ideas and make things happen

In the National Curriculum this is quite a broad strand that focuses not only on how ICT can help pupils get their ideas across but also sees the beginnings of programming, and experimenting with models or simulations to ask 'what if?' questions. Specifically they will:

- 'use text, tables, images and sound to develop their ideas';
- 'select from and add to information they have retrieved for particular purposes';
- 'plan and give instructions to make things happen';
- 'create, test, improve and refine sequences of instructions to make things happen and to monitor events and respond to them';
- 'try things out and explore what happens in real and imaginary situations';
- 'use simulations and explore models to answer "What if?" questions, to investigate and evaluate the effect of changing values and to identify patterns and relationships'.

In the classroom this means children will be working in a variety of ways, not just to present ideas in different ways such as texts or presentations, but also programming both on screen and with simple robots, as well as trying out different ideas to see what happens.

Developing ideas

This aspect of the ICT curriculum is about learning the power of the computer for creative activities as well as how everything works, from which key to press to changing font size and drawing and editing images. Pupils learn how to do the individual tasks of writing, drawing and recording sounds as well as combine these for different tasks. This area of the ICT curriculum is one where the skills learnt in the computer suite are readily transferred to many other tasks throughout the timetable. Gradually pupils use more complex tools through doing more demanding tasks.

Creating text

To begin with, children will type short words or phrases, such as their name, and print them out. They might also use a word-bank, which is an on-screen vocabulary list that you can select from simply by pointing and clicking. At this

MAIN IDEAS

We can use ICT to create, edit and manipulate text, images and sounds. These can be combined to present our ideas to others.

USEFUL VOCABULARY

Word processing: key, align, centre, backspace, spacebar, clip art, cut, copy, paste, delete, enter/return, font, highlight

Graphics: brush tool, clip art, fill, icon, re-size, frame, scanner, select, spray can

Others: import/export, insert, hyperlink, sequence, sample

TRANSFERABLE SKILLS

Using the keyboard correctly.

Cutting, copying and pasting.

Re-formatting and resizing text and images.

Creating images and recording sounds.

Combining text, graphics, and sounds.

---

stage pupils will begin to learn that text can be different sizes and colours. You can point out the posters and labels around the classroom and talk about why they use different formats for their lettering.

As pupils progress they will learn that, unlike when handwriting, text on a computer screen can be easily added to or edited in other ways. They need to learn to use the spacebar and the shift keys to write sentences accurately, and the backspace and delete keys to make corrections. As they move the cursor so they will be able to type anywhere within their writing. Then there is the enter key, more properly called the return key (from the carriage return lever on a typewriter), which is used to make new paragraphs or create lists.

Alongside these basic skills of word-processing they will also be learning the fundamental skills of drawing and editing graphics. These include drawing lines with the pencil and brush tools, creating shapes, filling areas with the fill tool, and using the spray can.

Once they have grasped the fundamentals of writing and drawing on screen they can begin to move things around. In a word-processor this is easily practised by putting a number of jumbled sentences on screen then asking children to put them in the correct order. Instructions work well for this, perhaps how to make a jam sandwich or log on to the computer. An activity such as this easily fits in with objectives in literacy lessons. Other ways of using the computer in this way could be to write a piece of text with no punctuation and put the marks in correctly (you could replace the punctuation marks with other characters to make it easier); or repeatedly use the word 'and' then replace it with full stops and commas. Another way of harnessing the editing power of the computer is to write without adjectives, or only using one such as 'nice', then improve the text with better words.

It often helps in activities such as these to use a pupil's own words, for example asking the pupil to dictate the sequence of instructions to make a sandwich. When looking at using adjectives they may already have written a piece that they could edit. In this way they have the support of knowing what it was they were wanting to say. They may also benefit from having paper copies to work with. When learning to cut and paste they can literally use scissors and glue to re-order before going onto the screen to do the same electronically. When checking the grammar of a text they can mark it up in pencil first while reading it aloud.

Combining text and graphics

As children begin to bring their skills together and combine text and graphics you can again show them everyday examples of books, magazines and posters. A simple first project is to make a greetings card, either drawing or finding an image then adding a suitable caption. Depending on their skills and the complexity of the task you could use clip art rather than drawings, and a word-bank to create phrases.

Later on, these are the sorts of skills pupils will use to create newsletters and front pages from papers. Here different styles and sizes of fonts will combine with drawings, photos and charts to present information about all sorts of topics. Typically this might be to give contemporary accounts of historical events, although it might also be to report on a school trip or the retelling of a story. However, images can be used to illustrate many different texts, including science or geography projects. When discussing a healthy diet examples of foodstuffs can be found on the internet, or when comparing different places to live photos can be downloaded to help explain and illustrate points.

At this level of work it will be appropriate to introduce the spellchecker. While introducing it too soon can get in the way of writing (see the later Literacy section), accuracy is important when producing some documents such as newspapers or web pages. Again, this can be illustrated with real-life examples, asking children if they can find mistakes and why it is important for readers that spellings are correct.

Creating graphics

Progression in the use of graphics packages will see pupils start to look at patterns with shapes, beginning with reflection or symmetry tools, making repeating patterns, either using a stamp tool, or creating their own drawing then selecting and copying it before repeatedly pasting.

The sort of activity shown in Figures 4.1 and 4.2 might fit in with a mathematics project, such as studying Islamic patterns, which are entirely formed along geometric lines.

It also fits in with the art curriculum. Pop art in particular uses repeating patterns with different degrees of shading. Other tools can be used to 'copy' the

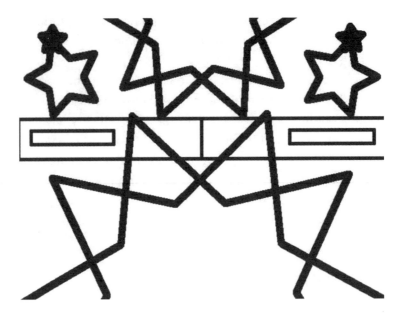

Figure 4.1 Stamp created with Blackcat artist

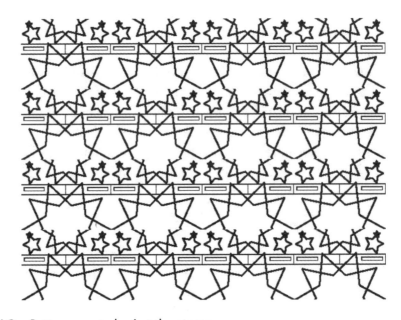

Figure 4.2 Pattern created using the stamp

work of some pop artists: for example, the spray can for Jackson Pollock's 'drip' paintings, the line, shape and fill tools for Mondrian's 'grid' paintings and the cut-and-paste tools for Dali's surrealist collages.

Using sounds

As well as manipulating images, pupils can experiment with sounds in a number of ways. For a start there are simple programs that use icons to represent individual notes or musical phrases, these can be arranged in short sequences, sometimes looped to be repetitive, and experimented with in different ways. Pupils can:

- choose four icons or phrases and try different orders;
- swap the icons for others;
- substitute different instruments;
- change the tempo;
- set lyrics to their phrases;
- improvise a percussion background;
- record a soundtrack for an animation.

Throughout these activities they will be critically evaluating what they are doing and modifying it. You can support them by asking a range of questions.

'What does that remind you of?'
'How does it make you feel? How might it make other people feel?'
'Is there anything you want to change?'
'Why do you prefer this one?'

They can also use an electronic keyboard experimentally, recording phrases, changing voices, adding backing tracks and exploring the possibilities. As they begin to understand how music can affect mood so they can create soundtracks to accompany other pieces of work. This will work particularly well with animations or short films, however they can also create backing tracks for multimedia presentations or even mood music for stories they have written. This is relatively easy in programs such as MSWord or PowerPoint where sounds can be added through the Insert menu.

Combining different media

This is particularly useful higher up the school when pupils will be expected to put sound, text, images and even film and animations together in presentations. Here they will need to show that they have a sense of their audience and that what they have created is fit for its purpose.

A useful starting point is to do some planning away from the computer. This can take the form of a brainstorm activity or mindmapping. Each topic can be written on an individual piece of paper, spread out on the desk or floor, and string used to show the links. While planning their presentation the pupils need to think about the number of ways that it can be presented. If the topic was local history for instance, then as well as interviews with local people they could add sounds that reflect the area, seagulls for a seaside town, aircraft near airports, and birdsong in the country, perhaps. They could also add songs that have a local significance. In the process of creating such a presentation they will be bringing together all the skills they have learnt in order to be creative with ICT as they have progressed through the school. Technically they will also be including transitions and animations to move the presentation on, and colours and backgrounds to create distinctive styles.

Making things happen

MAIN IDEAS

Through modelling and simulation ICT can be used to experiment with both real and fantasy situations where we can make and test predictions.

Machines follow commands and we can control them through sequences of instructions that can be repeated and amended to create procedures. Inputs and outputs can be varied to change how the computer works.

USEFUL VOCABULARY

model, simulation, instruction, sequence, order, procedure, command, program, floor turtle, control device, sensor, data-logging, monitoring, data, spreadsheet, cell, formula, sum.

TRANSFERABLE SKILLS

Controlling a mouse, including dragging and dropping.

Understanding directions such as left, right and straight on.

Using numbers and standard units.

Creating and interpreting graphs.

Entering formulas for basic operations, including adding and subtracting.

This aspect of ICT is about taking control and experimenting with different inputs and outputs, including giving instructions, using sensors and changing different bits of data to see what happens. It falls broadly into two areas: controlling and programming robots and turtles, both on screen and in real situations, and using models and simulations.

Simple modelling

When they first begin to 'model' with a computer, children may be simply working with ready-made elements to produce pictures. This could be by selecting fish and creating a virtual fish tank; building up a scene of a park or a zoo; or putting clothes on a figure. They will be using a computer simulation to depict real-life situations. It is important to help them to make the distinction, to discuss the differences, how when working in the two dimensions of a computer screen things are easier to manipulate, and will react differently to real life. For instance, when dressing a doll it can be difficult to get the sleeves over the hands. When you hide something behind a cushion on a computer screen it doesn't bulge. In a virtual fish tank the inhabitants swim backwards and forwards not round and round.

There are advantages of using a computer though. It is possible to try out different variations and combinations quickly and easily. Which clothes look best? Where in a playground can the swings go? How many big fish and smaller fish can fit in the tank comfortably? These can all be asked as 'what if' questions.

'What if I try the blue trousers and the yellow scarf?'

'What if I put the slide on the hill?'

'What if I make the silver fish much bigger?'

With a computer it is possible to alter things if we want to explore another possibility, and another, and another, and another. As children go through the school so the possibilities will become more complex. At first they might use games to simulate real-life situations. These can vary from simple online ones to more complex, commercial games.

One example of a simple simulation on the internet is 'Lemonade Stand'. There is more than one version of this, but they all follow the same format whereby players run a drinks stand for a given period, usually a month. During this time they have to make as much money as they can, they have to buy ingredients, create a recipe and set a price. In some versions they can also decide where to set up their stand, at the beach or in the mall for instance. The game itself also has some variables including the weather and the number of people around. As the pupils play so they will experiment with finding a recipe that can be sold for the best price that people are prepared to pay.

Modelling with a spreadsheet

From using simple models pupils can move on to creating spreadsheet models. You can start by thinking about the lemonade recipe and how much it might cost to make a litre. It may be easiest at this point to use a known recipe rather than try to create one, such as one lemon and 100 grams of sugar per litre of water. As the quantity of sugar is one tenth of a bag they will need to do some simple calculations to work out the price of one litre. From here a number of other questions can be asked.

'What is the cost of one cup of lemonade?'

'How many lemons will be needed to make 1 litre? 10 litres?'

'What is the production cost of one litre of lemonade? What is it for ten litres?'

At each point the pupils will need to be shown how to enter formulas into a spreadsheet to perform the calculations. Remember most spreadsheet software needs an equals sign, '=' at the beginning of any calculations and that divide is represented by a slash, '/', and multiply by an asterisk, '*'.

This exercise can be developed by setting up a virtual café. Everyone can be issued with a price list and asked to calculate the cost of a family meal, or a children's party, for a set sum. Again you change the variables; the number of people coming to eat, the cost of the menu items, the amount of money available. As each changes, the pupils will be able to see the effect on the spreadsheet as a whole.

To extend the exercise, you can use the model of the cost of lemonade only using other menu items, such as a cup of tea, coffee, or hot chocolate, or include foods such as chips, pizzas or hamburgers. The complexity of the item and the number of ingredients will help to differentiate the tasks for the pupils. For instance, a hamburger might only require a burger and a bun, or it might be made from minced meat, chopped onion, lettuce, tomato and dressing. It is also possible to think about variations such as chicken burgers, halal options and vegetarian alternatives. In this way the whole class can contribute to working out the costs of running a small café and the profit margin for different prices.

A more advanced form of modelling involves abstract problems such as mathematical shapes. For example, you can ask the pupils to find the area of a rectangle, given a fixed perimeter. If a rectangle has a total perimeter of 20 metres, what is the greatest area it can have? The sides can be anything between 1 and 9 metres long. The pupils need to add the length of all four sides to find the perimeter and multiply two sides to find the area. You can see the results of the calculations in Figure 4.3.

In order to solve the problem pupils could type in every number and every formula however once the first row is in place it is possible to set up the spreadsheet to do the rest of the work.

We know that the opposite sides are the same length. The length of side C will be the same as side A; D will be the same as B. The total distance around the perimeter will be A+B+C+D; the area will be A*B.

In the second row the length of A will be one greater and B will be one less. If the pupils started with sides of 1 and 9, rather than type in the numbers 2 and 8 we can tell the computer to add 1 to the first cell and take 2 away from the second. It already knows the other two sides are the same as the first two and so these change automatically, as do the calculations for perimeter and area. You can see the same spreadsheet with the formula visible in Figure 4.4.

While this may seem complicated you can see that the whole set of calculations can be done with only two numbers being entered. If the teacher wants to work with a different perimeter only the first two numbers need to be changed.

It is possible to try larger and smaller perimeters and, with some additional columns, work with 3D shapes.

	A	B	C	D	E	F
	Side a	side b	side c	side d	total perimeter m	total area m²
1						
2	1	9	1	9	20	9
3	2	8	2	8	20	16
4	3	7	3	7	20	21
5	4	6	4	6	20	24
6	5	5	5	5	20	25
7	6	4	6	4	20	24
8	7	3	7	3	20	21
9	8	2	8	2	20	16
10	9	1	9	1	20	9
11	10	0	10	0	20	0
12						

Figure 4.3   Excel spreadsheet showing sides of a rectangle

	A	B	C	D	E	F
	Side a	side b	side c	side d	total perimeter m	total area m²
1						
2	1	9	=A2	=B2	=SUM(A2:D2)	=A2*B2
3	=A2+1	=B2-1	=A3	=B3	=SUM(A3:D3)	=A3*B3
4	=A3+1	=B3-1	=A4	=B4	=SUM(A4:D4)	=A4*B4
5	=A4+1	=B4-1	=A5	=B5	=SUM(A5:D5)	=A5*B5
6	=A5+1	=B5-1	=A6	=B6	=SUM(A6:D6)	=A6*B6
7	=A6+1	=B6-1	=A7	=B7	=SUM(A7:D7)	=A7*B7
8	=A7+1	=B7-1	=A8	=B8	=SUM(A8:D8)	=A8*B8
9	=A8+1	=B8-1	=A9	=B9	=SUM(A9:D9)	=A9*B9
10	=A9+1	=B9-1	=A10	=B10	=SUM(A10:D10)	=A10*B10
11	=A10+1	=B10-1	=A11	=B11	=SUM(A11:D11)	=A11*B11

Figure 4.4   Excel spreadsheet showing sides of a rectangle, with formulas

Control

Control is the aspect of the ICT curriculum considered the most difficult to teach, perhaps because it requires the greatest degree of technical knowledge. It involves controlling machines, both real and virtual, through working out and inputting sequences of instructions, often using commands that are unique to this activity. It is probably the area that schools ask for most support from advisors, so it may well be the area that pupils need the most support to achieve in.

Although it can be a demanding area, learning how to give clear instructions in precise language is a useful skill for children to have. So is problem solving and thinking logically, which help to develop higher order thinking skills. Teaching control is well worth the investment needed to do it successfully.

To begin with, control is fairly straightforward. It is about how we use everyday technology and the need to work in a particular sequence to make things work. At first you might simply point out the need to turn some toys on and off, that others give varied reactions depending upon where you press them, and more complex ones might run through a series of actions. From here you can introduce the idea of having control over electronic devices. It is important to talk about how this happens in our everyday lives, from turning on a kettle, adjusting the setting on the toaster, and choosing the programme on the washing machine, to programming the video and making photocopies. With all of these activities we are taking control, determining the outputs through giving the machine commands to follow.

Having thought about toys and everyday technology, children can put control into practice, perhaps by creating and playing back a voice recording or a short piece of film using one of the many tools now designed for young children. In either instance they will need to understand the sequence of buttons to push to both record and playback, and even how to download this to a computer using leads and appropriate software.

The idea of following instructions to make things happen can be developed through other aspects of the curriculum too. Instructional writing is a good example, with pupils creating step by step guides for a variety of tasks, making a piece of toast, washing hands, or getting dressed for instance. In PE they can tell each other how to cross a space or negotiate an obstacle course, blindfolded even. At this point the idea of standard measures can be introduced, a concept necessary for working with programmable robots.

A group of pupils standing in a straight line when asked to take ten steps forward will inevitably end up in a ragged line as their steps will be of differing sizes. When first using a floor robot (often referred to as a 'turtle'), it is important to demonstrate that the step sizes are the same every time. That one of the advantages of using the robot is this certainty. A good activity to demonstrate this principle is to play skittles. Start by throwing balls to knock them down, then try using a ramp (if you have one) to at least get them travelling in the same direction every time, even if the force and distance vary. Then introduce the turtle. At first this might simply be getting it to travel sufficient distance to reach the skittles. Once this is achieved greater complexity can be introduced, spreading the skittles out so that the turtle has to turn and move again to get them all.

A number of activities will build on and develop the skills used. Routes of increasing complexity, such as obstacle courses, pausing, or playing musical notes at different points can be introduced. Pupils will also need to record their sequences of instructions and test them out, the first steps in writing computer programs. Again this could be in other lessons, asking them to write instructions to move from their desk to someone else's. While they could use everyday language such as 'right', 'left', and 'straight on', they might also use symbols such as arrows to achieve this.

Programming a real floor turtle will lead to programming a virtual one on a computer screen. There are a number of different programs that do this, several of which begin with users selecting symbols to build the process. However, the principle behind all of them is a programming language called 'Logo' which was developed by Seymour Papert in the 1970s. He did this to support Constructivist ideas about education, that people construct their own knowledge and understanding through the experiences they have and that the role of teachers is to provide useful, meaningful tasks to help this to happen. The basis of Logo is to explore how it works through different challenges and problems.

This idea has been taken up and developed by many educational software producers, although the original program can be downloaded for free from the internet. However, its descendants may seem more user friendly. As Logo is a particular programming language certain commands may need to be learnt in order to use it. Some of these are simply abbreviations:

Forward – Fd
Back – Bk
Turn Right – Rt
Turn Left – Lt
Clear Screen – Cs

Others are instructions:
Home – takes the turtle back to the starting point in the centre of the screen
Pendown – lets the turtle draw
Penup – stops drawing.

These commands can be used together, so 'fd 100 rt 90 fd 100 rt 90 fd 100 rt 90 fd 100 rt 90' would draw a square. The sides would be 100 on-screen turtle steps long, which on screen are a lot smaller than on a floor turtle, with 90 being the number of degrees to turn right.

At first it will be helpful to give pupils sheets of written instructions to follow to build shapes, although some will very quickly begin to vary the lengths of sides and degree of turns to see what happens. The principles learnt in mathematics about the number of degrees in a shape can be discussed as part of this experimentation.

As you can see, the process of drawing a regular shape involves repetition. The instructions can be simplified by telling Logo to 'repeat'. This time a square will be 'Repeat 4 [fd 100 rt 90]'. The square brackets around the instructions tell Logo what to repeat. From here the next step is to build 'procedures', this is when a set of instructions is named so simply typing in 'Square' will automatically draw one, with variations being the length of the sides or the pen colour.

As you can see, using Logo, or similar packages, can develop from quite a simple activity to one requiring a new language and concepts to be learnt. From creating simple shapes pupils can then be challenged to write their initials, make simple drawings or even complex mathematical shapes.

The programming skills learnt in this virtual environment can be applied to practical activities such as building model traffic lights, lighthouses or burglar alarms. Here specialist hardware will be necessary which usually links up to a computer to be programmed, unlike floor turtles where this is generally done directly into the machine.

A fairly well known example of this specialist, computer controlled, hardware, is 'Lego Robolab'. Familiar plastic bricks can be put together to create programmable machines by using a central 'RCX Brick' that receives commands from the computer via an infrared tower. The control brick can take up to five different programs at one time which will control up to three outputs, and respond to three separate inputs.

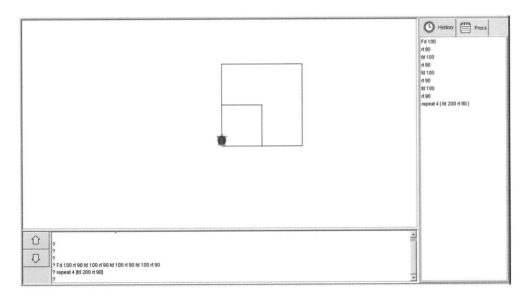

Figure 4.5 Drawing a square with Blackcat Logo

The most commonly used outputs are motors or light bulbs, although these bricks can also be programmed to play music. The inputs could be sensors that respond to touch, light or sound. Fortunately the kits come with step by step visual instructions to help pupils build the initial models, although they may go on to create their own. Typically the models will be around a theme. In the fairground kit pupils build bumper cars that change direction when they hit each other, or build a ghost train which replicates a customer going round a circuit while various nasties jump out at them.

Other control boxes let pupils apply their understanding of sequencing instructions and creating procedures for different purposes, such as using heat and light sensors to control the ventilation of a greenhouse, or pressure pads to create a burglar alarm.

The important thing in using these devices is the process of developing and testing instructions to achieve a desired outcome. While building a car-park barrier that counts the number of times it lifts and will stay shut if there is no more space, until the exit barrier is lifted, seems a long way from following instructions to move through a maze drawn on the hall floor, the common theme is that of giving precise instructions in a logical sequence, sometimes in a language that needs to be learnt.

Much of what children learn through these aspects of the National Curriculum is the nuts and bolts of ICT in schools, both in finding out about computers as a subject as well as in using them as tools for learning across the curriculum. In turn many other aspects of those subjects can be called upon to help teach ICT.

Helping children exchange and share information

The 'C' in ICT stands for communication, which is what this strand of the National Curriculum emphasises, the ability to both give information in ways that are appropriate to the other person and receive and retrieve it by electronic means. Specifically, pupils study:

- 'how to share and exchange information in a variety of forms';
- 'to be sensitive to the needs of the audience';
- to 'think carefully about the content and quality when communicating information'.

These are all objectives that are not about ICT alone, but about many aspects of schoolwork. As with much of the ICT curriculum, skills learnt here can be applied across the timetable.

How we might exchange and share information

MAIN IDEAS

With computers we can use information in many forms – words, pictures, sounds – to get a message across. These can be used separately or combined and manipulated to satisfy the needs of different audiences and purposes.

USEFUL VOCABULARY

email, attachment, address book, accuracy, bias, error, spellchecker, audience

TRANSFERABLE SKILLS

Use the range of keys on the keyboard and common tools in word-processing, graphics packages, and multimedia packages.

Send and receive emails and find information from different sources, including books, electronic media, interviews and surveys.

Use inputs such as scanners, cameras and sensors.

Presenting information

Throughout the ICT curriculum pupils will use a particular application to produce documents for an audience. For example, they might use:

- word-processing applications to produce letters, stories, reports, instructions, recounts, assessments;
- drawing and graphics packages to produce documents with photos, drawings, maps, wrapping paper, illustrations;
- analysis and graphing packages to produce results of surveys, outcomes from experiments, representations of data capture;
- music packages to produce songs, raps, jingles, background music.

They might also combine their products:

- newspapers, adverts and posters;
- presentations and web pages;
- greetings cards, invitations and certificates;
- illustrated reports of school visits and suggestions to the school council or governors on ways to improve the school environment with photographs and survey results.

Through their school careers children create documents and images of increasing complexity. At first they might create simple documents and drawings, perhaps using a word-bank to write a sentence and even the stamp tool in a drawing package to create a pattern. Then they might add a caption to a drawing, or write one for a photo from a school visit, to a farm perhaps, saying what is happening. There are a number of packages around now that even infants can use to add animations and sound effects to stories, giving them a multimedia element that used to be introduced much further up the school.

Children will also be working with sounds, listening to recordings to see what they can find out, but also beginning to make their own recordings. With easy to use software they can begin to create their own music, experimenting with different rhythms, tempos and instruments.

Desktop publishing

It may well be that skills are applied in other subjects. In history they may be asked to create a newspaper front page for an historical event, such as the Gunpowder Plot. They will need to be introduced to the conventions of newspaper layout: the use of different fonts, of varying sizes, and images with captions, to draw the reader in to the story, emphasising the style of the writing and the audiences' needs.

Survey information can be used to inform and illustrate points in a report to the school council. This could be a pie chart of pupil choices for healthy school dinners, or a bar chart showing water collected from a leaking roof each time it rains. Here the language of the report will be more formal, with particular conventions such as bullet points and numbered paragraphs.

When completing such tasks pupils will become aware of the accuracy necessary for such publications. You can begin by showing them examples of printed documents, such as magazines and promotional flyers, and asking them to find errors, then discuss why there are so few. Help them to understand that accuracy in language means that people will understand the text and minimise confusion.

Writing for websites

Many schools now involve pupils in developing their websites. This requires yet another set of conventions. Web pages are usually written with short paragraphs, designed to convey a message very quickly as people are used to surfing the net for information and then moving on. The content needs to be clear and concise. Children will appreciate this from their own use of the internet. They will probably already be familiar with icons, buttons and hyperlinks. Even very young children may already be visiting favourite sites to play games. And older ones may be downloading music onto their MP3 players. This experience will give them a good sense of what successful web pages should look like. You can draw on their own understanding to help them to design their web pages.

Creating websites can be a messy business though, especially if pupils have created lots of links and pages that branch out in all sorts of directions. However, many of the brainstorming and mindmapping programs around now can help pupils think about the links between topics and create an outline of a site. They can fill in detail afterwards.

Mindmaps in themselves, though, are becoming widely recognised as publications in their own right, combining text, images and graphics to stimulate creativity and learning. They can be created to be interactive on the computer and then printed out and pasted on the wall.

It is important that pupils recognise that publication need not necessarily involve paper. Web pages and presentations can be just as valid a way of getting a message across.

New tools in learning

Technology is changing rapidly, which is having an impact on what we can do in the classroom. While video cameras have been with us for a while, the ease with which we can edit footage and distribute the results is comparatively new. As well as producing written work pupils are increasingly making films about what they are doing in class. In science, for instance, a demonstration on video of the principles of hydraulics is a more certain way of finding out just what a pupil has understood than a written explanation. Films can be quickly and easily burnt on DVDs or even distributed over the internet.

Another possibility for exchanging and sharing information is the use of 'blogging' and 'podcasts'. The first are usually in the form of online diaries. While commercial blogging sites are not particularly attractive as educational tools because of the advertising on them and the lack of editorial control, it is possible to set up blogs on school sites. Each child can be given their own space to record ideas, add images or examples of work, and link to favourite places, such as TV programmes, places they have visited, or other children's pages. An important aspect of blogging is interactivity, so there also needs to be room for readers' comments, either through a notice board or email links.

Podcasting can seem technically demanding, however a number of companies are now producing child-friendly software to support it. Essentially it is a means of making a personal broadcast, usually just with sound but increasingly with video and photos, which other people can download and enjoy. As a means of developing language skills it offers exciting possibilities. Pupils can make radio broadcasts for others to listen too. To do this they will need to think about how to convey a sense of their surroundings, the essential information a listener will need, and how to make what they say interesting enough to keep someone else engaged.

Using email

Electronic messaging is another form of exchanging and sharing information. Email is becoming very widely used so children need to understand what it is and how it works, particularly as there are some risks attached to communicating with the wider world. Generally all email communication by children in school should:

- be open, that is anyone should be able to read anything someone else is sending from a classroom computer;
- use addresses from educational providers, such as the school, local regional broadband consortium or commercial company;
- not use web-based email such as Hotmail or Yahoo.

Children need to be taught that if they ever have concerns when they are online they should tell an adult. While the risks of them being in touch with a predatory adult are very small they are also quite real, so in schools we need to take them seriously.

When learning to email, children can find it fun and interesting to contact children in other schools and find out about them. However, some software, such as '2Email', is designed to run across a school network, with children simply communicating with their friends. This simulates the system without there being any risk of messages going astray. Once the basics are grasped, contact can begin with children in other schools. In this situation it is fine to swap personal information, in fact it is often the purpose of the contact. Messages can be linked with a curriculum topic such as looking at different environments. Inner city children can describe their area to pupils in another part of the country, even abroad, or ask them to complete a survey to compare favourite foods or pastimes.

Pupils in one school can send a teddy bear through the post to pupils in another school as a means of communication. The teddy bear is used as a courier, to pass messages back and forth. Most schools now have contacts with teachers from other countries so this is easily arranged. As well as written messages, photos can be attached to emails to show where teddy is. The children will also need to learn to attach files to their own messages to send information to other people.

It's happening all the time

A large part of what happens in classrooms is the exchange and sharing of information. It is the essence of teaching. The adults convey information to the pupils who demonstrate that they have received and understood it by giving it back in different forms. ICT opens up the ways in which this is possible. Not only can pupils create paper-based documents, they can create electronic ones, to be seen on a computer or television. While pupils need to appreciate the possibilities that ICT offers, and be aware that these tools are part of the curriculum subject, a lot of the time the technology will have become invisible, simply the tool for the job at hand. This is when it has truly become embedded.

Helping children review, modify and evaluate work as it progresses

One of the characteristics of computers is provisionality: everything done can be undone, redone and done differently. It is endlessly changeable, so editing, refining and repurposing can become integral to the way we work with them. In the National Curriculum children are expected to:

- review what they and others have done;
- describe and talk about the effectiveness of their work;
- compare it with other methods;
- consider the effect on others;
- talk about how they could improve future work.

As you can see, the intention is for pupils to critically evaluate what they, and others, have done – what they have made as well as how they made it – and articulate this evaluation. Clearly a large part of this will be the way they talk about their use of ICT in their work, something that is integral to the supporting role of the teaching assistant.

MAIN IDEAS

Computers can help us to develop our thoughts as we use them to experiment and test our ideas. We need to look at work objectively, against the brief for the task, to determine whether it is sufficient for its purpose and intended audience.

USEFUL VOCABULARY

accuracy, spellcheck, edit, sequence, information, classify, data, predict, hypothesis, test

TRANSFERABLE SKILLS

All editing skills: cutting and pasting, dragging and dropping, re-sizing, re-formatting, saving in different versions, spellchecking, cropping, animating, changing tempo (in music editing) and so on.

The essence of this aspect is the ability to critically evaluate: for pupils to look at their own and others' work and ask whether it is what is needed or can it be improved. While this might be thought of as fairly subjective, there are ways in which we can make it less so. Some things, such as the particular shade of blue used as the background to a home-made logo, may simply be a question of taste. However, we could also ask about contrasting and complementary colours, and take into account the needs of people with visual impairments.

When looking at others' work, pupils need to be sensitive to the potential for any criticism to be taken personally. In a lot of classrooms children are taught particular ways of making sensitive comments. For instance, they are taught to begin by stating what they like and making a statement that is not personal:

'I like the way you have used the spray tool.'

'It's really good how the snail crawls in to the scene.'

'If this was my picture I would make the sky lighter because I think you could see the bird better then.'

Pupils also need to make sure that their work is accurate. In part they can do this using the tools of the computer. Most applications have a built in spellchecker, and some have grammar checkers too, although what these pick up is not always obvious and are sometimes simply a matter of personal style.

When using databases, pupils can be shown how to include criteria, so that they don't enter inappropriate values, such as letters in number fields or numbers that are too big or too small. They also need to be taught to question whether an answer is feasible. Is it possible that all the girls in the school have bigger feet than all the boys, for instance? As part of this process they may find they have to ask better questions, and to discriminate between 'open' and 'closed' ones; that is, questions that can be answered freely and ones which have a restricted number of answers such as 'yes' or 'no', 'boy' or 'girl', or a list of colours or foods.

Anomalies can show up when figures have been converted into charts. A blip on a bar chart or a sudden spike on a line graph may be a sign that data is inaccurate and needs to be checked. While working with charts it is also important to choose the right one. A pie chart will show proportions but not progression over time, so while it might show the number of days in a month that have been sunny it can't tell the story of the temperature change on each day.

On some occasions change is integral to the activity. When modelling, pupils will ask 'what if' questions. They will create and test hypotheses, then alter the model to see what happens. In the lemonade stand simulation, for example (see Chapter 4), they might ask:

'What if we use fewer lemons in our recipe?'

'What if we lower the price?'

'What if we set up nearer the car park?'

Similarly when working with a turtle, on the floor or on screen, pupils might try out different ideas. These could be a set of directions that give the shortest route between places, or the number of degrees that are necessary on each turn to draw a regular hexagon.

While pupils may evaluate and assess their own work right across the curriculum, opportunities for amending, experimenting and trying different ideas are greatly enhanced when using computers. The skill that staff need is helping them to evaluate and assess effectively.

CHAPTER 7

What is a 'breadth of study'?

There are many and varied new, electronic technologies available to us, with a host of different uses, some of which were not even thought of when the National Curriculum was first written. Having a 'breadth of study' is to make sure children experience a variety of these technologies, for a range of different purposes, and that they appreciate the role that ICT now plays in our lives.

Specifically the National Curriculum wants them to:

- work with 'a range of information', considering its 'characteristics and purposes';
- work with others to 'explore a variety of information sources and ICT tools';
- investigate and compare the 'uses of ICT inside and outside school'.

This may seem a rather vague and unspecific list, but it is impossible to encapsulate all the opportunities, tasks and activities that ICT could be put to within a pupil's time in primary school. The intention is to get school staff to think about the things they and their pupils can do with ICT and let pupils experience as wide a spectrum as possible.

Giving breadth when 'Finding things out'

There is a danger of considering this strand of the National Curriculum to be entirely about electronic sources. However, as we have seen from the section about teaching this aspect of ICT, the sources need to be a lot broader. They could include:

- the internet;
- CD-ROMs;
- DVDs;
- film clips and animations;
- newspapers and magazines;
- books, especially dictionaries, encyclopaedias, atlases and non-fiction works;
- surveys and questionnaires, both face to face and on line;
- downloaded statistics such as those from the National Records Office;
- interviews, with parents, writers, politicians and each other;
- email communication with other children around the world;

- webcams;
- video-conferencing;
- trips out, walking around the neighbourhood, or going to places of interest;
- visits to virtual museums.

A lot of these are activities that either don't need a computer or won't take place in ICT lessons. What you will do is help make the connection with the use of technology and help pupils to evaluate, interrogate and validate it all.

The first information sources that children encounter might be photos, sounds and symbols rather than text or numbers. Many of them will have heard parents talking about digital cameras and digital photos, which is an opportunity to talk about storing images and putting them on a computer rather than using a film, making them aware of the everyday use of technology around them. Why did their parents take the photos? Is that different from why a digital camera might be used in class? But we also need to ask them to think about the content of the photo. What can we learn from it? Was it a special occasion? How can we tell? We might be able to tell how long ago it was taken because of the style of the clothes, although it might have been from a booth at a theme park where the subjects can dress up in all sorts of outfits. You can link this possibility to children's own dressing-up activities and talk about the difference between pretending and what is real. There may be other clues in a photo, such as the pose, or the décor, or maybe the date is written on the back.

Children can also use the internet as an information source, to search for similar scenes to compare. Here we may begin to question the validity of the source – that is, were these photos put here by someone we can trust? Some will have been put there by people researching their family tree – they will have no reason to mislead but you may need to point out if they are from another place or culture. Other photos could be historical re-enactments, perhaps for television programmes, in which case they are contemporary and 'pretend'. You can talk to the children about what other information is on the web pages to help you decide which is which. Questions to ask might include:

'How do you know that?'
'Does anybody else know anything different?'
'How can we find out?'
'What other sources could we use?'
'What questions can we ask?'
'Who is giving us this information?'
'How can we tell that this is a reliable source?'

Sometimes the source can be a firsthand one, for example the children themselves or people they have contacted directly and interviewed or given a questionnaire to.

A useful way for pupils to start doing surveys is by looking at data that already exists, for example fields in a table on mini-beasts or graphs and charts from a nationally published opinion poll. The BBC Newsround website has ongoing polls in their 'Vote' section, with charts showing winners for things such as films and sports stars. Pupils can see how polls are presented, and question the validity of results, considering issues such as multiple voting, sample size and how representative the respondents might be. These will be young people with easy internet access, is that true for many young people? Would those who can't get on the internet easily have voted the same way? By looking at other people's questioning and how the survey is conducted they can refine their own.

Similarly, they can work with more formal, structured databases, looking at both the questions that can be asked of them, and the questions that were asked to create them. This will help them to structure their own research. For instance, if they want to compare the number of legs on mini-beasts found when pond-dipping to the number found when turning over logs they need to include fields about the number of legs, and the place where the creature was found. However, a more sophisticated question, such as the depth in the water at which it was found, would also require the question 'How deep was it found?' and a field to store that information in. Then there is the problem of the type of information. Generally it will be either text or numbers. The search and sort techniques may vary for these different sorts of data, so pupils will need to make sure each field is of the correct type for the sort of query they will run, or question they will ask.

Giving breadth when 'Developing ideas'

The number of ways that technology helps us to express our ideas continues to grow. The most common way we do this is by writing with a computer – using a word-processing package. Other ways are:

- desktop publishing: combining text and images for greeting cards, posters and newsletters;
- creating multimedia presentations with text, images, sounds or video, some of which are designed to be seen on screen rather than in print.

More recent innovations are:

- digital photography: using the power of the computer to enhance, manipulate, and create with a camera;
- using video cameras: making films, documentaries, and animations;
- recording sounds: making or mixing music (even without instruments), interviewing people for authentic records of events and experiences;
- creating web pages: presenting yourself to the world;
- making a blog: using an online diary to record thoughts, feelings and events;
- creating podcasts: 'radio broadcasting over the internet', sometimes with images or video;
- creating charts and graphs: showing the results of enquiries.

To do these activities, pupils have to think through what they want to say and how they can get their message across most effectively. They also have to think about the needs of their audience and how best to meet them, which includes thinking about the language used, the choice and type of images and the presentation format: on screen or in print.

As well as considering the needs of other people when sharing their ideas, pupils will also benefit from working with each other. Often collaboration can help to refine and define what we want to say. Children need to experience this and some activities, such as making a video, are almost impossible to achieve without the help of other pupils, but even talking through a story idea can help to develop it. It is best to teach children the skill of positively critiquing other people's ideas so that they can best help each other rather than take it as an opportunity to establish a creative pecking order.

Giving breadth when 'Making things happen'

To make things happen in ICT, pupils need to understand how they control the technology in their own environment as well as take control of more specialist technology in lessons. The former could include:

- playing with electronic toys;
- using a photocopier;
- using a video camera;
- taking digital photos;
- selecting a starting point on a CD or DVD;
- driving a remote control car.

The latter is more sophisticated and could include:

- programming a floor turtle;
- programming a turtle on screen;
- creating programs on screen and then sending them to real devices, such as a robot, or programmable construction kit;
- using electronic sensors to record information;
- changing what devices do, such as opening and closing windows on models, depending on what information is sent to them.

Models and simulations

In primary school a model or simulation can take many forms. It may be populating a zoo on screen, using animal stamps and a background, using texture tools in an art program to explore different types of painting techniques or doing science experiments in a virtual laboratory. It could even be playing a commercial computer game as an entrepreneur to try to become a virtual millionaire or creating a spreadsheet to explore the number of rabbits that a particular bit of countryside will support given any number of lettuces or foxes. All of these are situations in which we can ask, 'what if?' questions, and test hypotheses, which we might do when working in science or mathematics, and when we do we can make the link with ICT and point out the similarities.

What is important is to give pupils the opportunity to experiment, to create hypotheses and to test these. At first this might be using a program to dress an on-screen cuddly toy. The experimentation might be to use clothing appropriate to the weather, season or occasion, such as rain gear or for going to a party. It could also be designing a T-shirt using a self-portrait and image handling software with various filters. Each pupil's outcome will be different because they are starting from a different image, and they can apply various effects such as kaleidoscopic ones, or particular colour tints. The focus should be on whether the final version is something that would look good on a T-shirt as they walk down the street. Graphics software will let them experiment with their original, asking 'What if I applied this effect?', or 'What if I make it brighter?'

With a computer game or spreadsheet model pupils are able to experiment with taking charge and making decisions. In games that simulate running attractions such as 'Zoo Tycoon', or 'Rollercoaster Tycoon', they have to maximise visitors, control costs and make money.

Even when planning a school visit pupils can try different variables, asking, or being asked, questions that might make big differences to their calculations:

- If discounts are given for groups of ten, but only nine people are booked on the trip, how much cheaper will it be if they can persuade someone else to go?

- The coach will seat 53 people, what happens to the price if 55 book? What's the price of one double decker taking 74, compared to two singles?

- How is the price affected if you visit at weekends, or at less popular times of the year?

While the above are based on real situations it is also possible to model abstract concepts. For example, you can create polygons by changing the angles of the corners and lengths of sides in Logo. You can also test mathematical concepts. For example, you can find the number of squares on a standard chessboard (or on one that's shaped like a rectangle, or any quadrilateral) with a formula for this. Pupils would need to try different shapes to find patterns and test the formula. In either situation, the computer does the mathematics but the pupils work out the calculations that need doing. They also decide if the answers are reasonable. If not, the pupils need to revisit what they have asked the computer to do.

Giving breadth when 'Exchanging and sharing information'

There are now many ways in which we exchange and share information. Some of them have been with us for a long time, such as sending letters and producing newspapers. Others are still developing. Those that are based on new technologies include:

- fax
- email
- digital video
- video-conference
- webcam
- website
- podcast

- blog
- SMS text messaging
- videophone
- Wiki (a shared encyclopaedia)
- Bulletin board
- Newsgroup
- online messaging (such as MSN)
- web-based voice messaging
- MP3, DVD or CD players
- personal webspaces.

While we do not necessarily expect children to experience all of these in school (some we might discourage them from experiencing), they are all means of communicating that have come into existence in recent years. Some of them pupils experience anyway, especially with the growth of mobile phone ownership. However, if children aren't experiencing text or online messaging, we may want to give them that opportunity, just as we do with email. Likewise, we may not want them to freely use webcams in school for a number of reasons, including practicality and child-protection, but we might set up a video-conference to show them the possibilities.

As well as experiencing a range of ways of sharing and exchanging information (including electronic and paper-based media and talking and listening), pupils need to think about the nature of the information – not only the type it is but who made it (and made it available), why, and if it is reliable.

Information comes from many different categories, such as:

- first hand account;
- journalistic report;
- answers to a questionnaire;
- historical document;
- results of an investigation or experiment;
- rumour or speculation.

Some of these can be measurably proven to be true (results of investigations or experiments) while others might be given to bias (including some firsthand accounts). It can help to consider why the information is being presented. Is it to influence us in some way? Or maybe to entertain? Perhaps it is to prove a particular point of view. While children need to be able to trust information sources in order for them to be able to work with them, they also need to have the skills of critically appraising them. One way to do this is to take a news story and look at how it is presented in different papers, and on websites, both institutional ones and personal ones such as blogs. While the information central to the story might remain the same, the language used and the way it is presented can give the same facts a very different feel.

Giving breadth when 'Reviewing, modifying and evaluating work as it progresses'

As pupils carry out a particular task or complete some form of evaluation, whether formal or not, there are plenty of opportunities to think about how well it has been addressed. On some occasions you may want children simply to reflect on what they have done during a lesson, perhaps to consider whether there are improvements to be made but most importantly to recognise what they have learnt and achieved. On others you can share the National Curriculum levels with them and see where they think they are.

It is good practice to involve pupils in evaluating their work. This could be through the formal completion of an assessment sheet or diary, or by pulling the work up on an interactive whiteboard for the whole class to comment on. The key is to consider whether the learning objectives and intended outcomes have been met, and if so, how well. But that is not the only time that pupils will be approaching their work with a critical eye. A number of opportunities, varying in complexity and formality, will arise. These might include:

- looking at a poster they have created and considering what is the most eye-catching aspect of it;
- discussing the different purposes of pie charts, line graphs and bar charts and when we might use these, then creating examples of each from the same dataset to test which are the most useful;
- creating mock-up front pages for different newspapers and considering what sort of person might buy each;
- sharing a multimedia story on the interactive whiteboard and asking the class to say what they liked and how, if they had created it, they would change it;
- emailing their designs for a new playground to each other to ask who would like to play in it.

Pupils also need to learn to be discriminating about their use of ICT – when and whether to use it, which tool is the most appropriate, whether there is a better method. For instance, if they were organising a celebration of Christmas, Eid or Divali and inviting parents, governors and local dignitaries they would have a number of choices. They could:

- invite people verbally;
- send an email;
- post out invitations.

The first option is the most personal, but it is not certain that everyone who needed to know would get to hear about it. The second might be quickest but could seem too impersonal, might get overlooked, and won't reach people without email addresses. The third option is the most formal, but also the most conventional, the one most likely to reach recipients, and to be given proper consideration.

In this instance the message might be created on a computer but not sent via one. The next question then, is what program to use, a word-processor or a desktop publisher. Then comes the question of design: what information to include, how to lay it out, and any sort of illustrations. A number of designs could be created by individuals or small groups and discussed by the class as a whole. Throughout this process pupils will be considering what is the best way to go about the task, the appearance and content necessary to get the message across, and will be drawing up a number of drafts. And they will need to think about how well the product meets the needs of the task, both in terms of getting the message across, and in how it will be perceived by its audience, that is, the people who get the invitations.

This task has a clear, real-world purpose but others might be more abstract or imaginative. Comparing different brands of lemonade by compiling a database of their characteristics might require pupils to come up with criteria for grading taste, smell or colour, which are all difficult to define and experienced differently by each individual. Here they might record the taster's preferences under categories such as 'sweetness', 'lemonyness' and 'thirst quenching'. The challenge is to find ways of determining what makes up each of these characteristics and how they can be captured on a database. At the end of the process they can produce a questionnaire about what brands people like and hold a blind tasting, to compare the results of their investigation with pupils' perceptions. Here they can be considering whether the processes they developed to record the data have been sufficiently rigorous to answer the question. They might also want to discuss whether it is a question that can ever be accurately addressed, given our individual preferences.

Asking pupils to critically evaluate their work is common across the curriculum and goes on in many ways all the time, often without us realising that this is what is going on. With ICT the tasks and tools may be different, but the principles are not.

Overall, the objective of a broad use of ICT is to make children aware of the possibilities that this technology presents us, to offer them experiences of its use, and to understand its place in our everyday lives. Alongside this they will be developing the skills necessary to be effective users of it – from straightforward ones such as cutting and pasting, to more complex ones like mixing music and editing films. All the time, they will be thinking about what the purpose of the task is, asking whether they could be doing it better, and sharing their ideas with the rest of us in a way that we will find understandable.

Assessing ICT: how do we know what pupils have learnt?

We can think of assessment in different ways: giving pupils a level at the end of a unit or while they're actually working, to let them know how they are getting on and what they might do to get a better outcome. Essentially, we are making judgements, and those judgements need to be based on some idea of what pupils have achieved and there has to be some means of describing it.

There are two main ways that we assess pupils: summative and formative.

Summative assessment is when we give a child a level for what they have achieved. It is a snapshot of where they have got to at any particular point. We give them a grade, often a number such as a National Curriculum attainment target. We can think of it as a summary or summing up of what they have done. While this will be the responsibility of the class teacher, you may have worked more closely with children and will have a role in helping to evaluate just where they have got to. Summative assessment involves looking at the outcomes, at what a child has produced and measuring this in some way.

Formative assessment is ongoing. It is about focusing on the learning that is taking place and helping the child understand how they are getting on and what they need to do to improve. This is about the task and the way the child is approaching it. Here we would refer to the learning objectives and give the child guidance on how to achieve them. It is the sort of thing you probably do instinctively, helping to keep pupils focused on the job in hand. Formative assessment involves looking at the learning as it progresses, talking to pupils and giving feedback on how to improve.

Both summative and formative assessment play an important part in the classroom. You will probably find yourself more involved in formative than summative assessment, even though you may not realise it.

Summative assessment

It might help to think of this method of assessment as summarising achievements: we 'sum up' what a child has done. We evaluate their understanding and capabilities and give them some sort of level, a way of comparing current and previous attainment, and of judging performance against school, local and national standards.

The National Curriculum marks achievement through level descriptors in subject attainment targets. There are eight levels in each target as well as an exceptional performance level. There are also eight levels in the P scales, used for pupils who are unlikely to achieve above National Curriculum level 2 throughout their school careers ('P' stands for 'pre' National Curriculum). Most children in mainstream primary schools are somewhere between level 1 and level 4, with some at level 5.

While responsibility for assessing what level a child has reached rests with the class teacher, it is quite likely, as with other curriculum areas, that they will value your contribution to the process. It may also be helpful to you to understand how the decision was arrived at, and why children whose attainments may seem similar are thought to have achieved at different levels.

The key characteristics of the National Curriculum ICT level descriptors

The following are the key characteristics of the NC level descriptors. For the exact text, see the Appendix.

- Level 1: characterised by the use of ICT to explore options and make choices to communicate meaning. Pupils develop familiarity with simple ICT tools.

- Level 2: characterised by the purposeful use of ICT to achieve specific outcomes.

- Level 3: is characterised by the use of ICT to develop ideas and solve problems.

- Level 4: is characterised by the ability to combine and refine information from various sources.

- Level 5: characterised by combining the use of ICT tools within the overall structure of an ICT solution. Pupils critically evaluate the fitness for purpose of work as it progresses.

Each level builds upon the previous one, so for a child to be thought of as being at any particular level they need to have shown the characteristics of the previous ones in their work.

It may help to think about how you would describe the way pupils are working as a guide to the level they are at by looking at some of the language used in the descriptors. Here are some of the keywords and phrases for describing achievement in ICT:

- At level 1 they 'explore information from various sources . . . use ICT to work with text, images and sound . . . share their ideas . . . make choices . . . produce different outcomes . . . talk about their use of ICT'.

- At level 2 they 'organise and classify information . . . present their findings . . . enter, save and retrieve work . . . generate, amend and record . . . share ideas in different forms . . . plan and give instructions . . . describe the effects . . . explore what happens in real and imaginary situations . . . talk about their experiences . . . inside and outside school'.

- At level 3 they 'save information . . . use . . . stored information, following straightforward lines of enquiry . . . generate, develop, organise . . . share and exchange their ideas with others . . . control devices . . . achieve specific outcomes . . . use ICT-based models or simulations . . . solve problems . . . describe their use of ICT'.

- At level 4 they take 'care in framing questions when collecting, finding and interrogating information . . . interpret their findings, question plausibility . . . add to, amend and combine different forms of information . . . present information in different forms . . . are aware of the intended audience . . . exchange information and ideas with others . . . including . . . email . . . control events . . . sense physical data . . . use . . . models and simulations to explore patterns and relationships . . . make predictions about . . . consequences . . . compare their use of ICT with other methods'.

If you use the language from the level descriptors to describe what a child is doing in ICT you will more easily understand the levels being ascribed to the child.

Progression

If a child is simply exploring information they are likely to be at level 1. When they begin to organise that information they are moving to level 2, and as they use it to answer questions that they have generated they are at level 3. As they begin to think about how they frame their questions and analyse the information more thoroughly, they move on to level 4. Although these are the levels most children will be at in primary schools, some will not have attained as much, and others will have done better.

Pupils on the upper end of the P scales will 'gather information from different sources' (P7) and 'find similar information in different formats' (P8). Those at the upper end of the attainment tables for primary school – those reaching level 5 – will 'select the information they need for different purposes, check its accuracy and organise it in a form suitable for processing'.

The sort of progression seen here for 'Finding things out' can be found in all aspects of the National Curriculum and the QCA scheme of work. When 'Exchanging and sharing information', they will be progressing from selecting words from an on-screen word-bank, through combining text and graphics to make greetings cards, to creating multimedia presentations and videos. When 'Developing ideas and making things happen', they will progress from labelling with key words through to creating appropriate charts, as well as moving from dressing teddy on screen to changing data in a spreadsheet.

While it is possible to see progression here, the difficult thing is in giving it a level, in accurately measuring where a pupil is. It is not, as you can imagine, an exact science. Among the things teachers do is to set assessment activities based on the unit of work; keep portfolios of examples of pupils work for comparison; hold moderation meetings across the school to discuss and compare; talk to children about what they did and why.

There are examples of pupils' work, assessed at NC levels, on the National Curriculum in Action website (www.ncaction.org.uk).

Formative assessment

Formative assessment is concerned less with what the child has achieved and more with where they are on the learning journey – the places they have been to before and what they need to do to get to the next place. Teachers signpost learning by explaining what the task is, what the criteria for success are and how the different levels might be achieved. It is about checking where children are and guiding them on their way. Much of the activity in a plenary session at the end of a lesson is formative. Teachers ask pupils to show their work and talk about what they have done, or direct specific questions to different children to check that they have understood what they were doing.

How this works in practice

An example of how formative assessment works in practice can be seen in the activity of creating a multimedia presentation. This is in the QCA scheme of work for Year 6, but younger pupils are now doing this sort of activity as software for them and the activity becomes available.

The task is to create an information booth for an open evening, celebrating the school's achievements over the last year. It will be set up in the entrance hall for parents to browse as they wish. It will run on a touch screen so users will be able to make choices about what they want to know about and touch an on-screen button to access it.

There are several things that will need to be made clear to the pupils before they start:

- the target audience is parents visiting the school;
- they might not go through every slide available but just look at one or two on their way through the entrance hall;
- the content will need to be strongly visual as the soundtrack may not be easy to hear and users might not want to read much;
- there will need to be a 'home' button on every page so that each new user can start afresh.

The success criteria is that the presentation is:

- appropriate for the target audience as it retains their interest and meets their information needs;
- it uses appropriate language, images and sounds;
- it is easy to navigate;
- it works on a touch screen.

Pupils will work in groups to present different aspects of the school year for the information booth. They could work in different year groups, or by the events over the year such as sports day, the infant trip to the seaside, the Christmas Party. All of them will have access to a bank of images and be able to ask the teachers and other staff for their comments.

Some pupils produce a series of slides consisting of photos and captions, each of which changes to the next using a transition effect with sound. Users touch a button marked 'Next' to go to the next page.

Other pupils include images of children's work among the slides, with a voice-over commentary for each one. Users will sometimes be given a choice of which page they want to look at next.

The most advanced work includes images, examples of pupils' work and short video clips. Interviews with staff and children play as each slide opens or when an on-screen button is touched. Slides can be viewed in a number of sequences, which users choose from an on-screen menu.

In each of these cases the pupils have met the brief, but to different degrees. The outcomes themselves can be levelled, probably between levels 3 and 5, however the process will have required them to take a number of decisions, about content, navigation and presentation, as well as to have used a range of skills, including combining text, graphics and sound. They will also have recorded images and sounds, and considered the language they would use.

They will have had to ask and answer a number of questions while completing the task, including:

'What images best show the class or event off?'
'How will the slides link together, progressing from one to another, or with multiple links between them?'
'What captions will be needed? How much information will be in each one?'
'Where will the use of sound enhance the presentation, making it easier to understand or more engaging?'
'Should they use transition effects with sounds? If so which ones, the same all the way through or varied?'

Your role in this would be to help them to ask those questions and to decide how well they have answered them. For instance,

'Are the chosen photos clear, or would they be better cropped? How many images will be needed to tell the story of that event, or class?'
'Are the transitions there to enhance the presentation or just because they look snazzy?'
'Are the captions helpful? Do they give the user just the right amount of information?'
'Does the user need to click every time to move on, or can some of the transitions be timed to move on automatically?'

While the pupils look at how to achieve the required result, your role is to help them engage with the process in a more critical way and determine how well they are meeting the learning objectives and the success criteria.

Once the activity is completed you can help them to think about what they have achieved. You would help them to:

- identify their strengths and ways in which they can develop them;

- reflect on areas of weakness and how they can address these;

- find ways to improve their work.

You can help them state how well they think they have met the criteria, what they have learned, and how they would like to build on this in the future. You could use a self-assessment questionnaire, which would have questions like:

What did you include in your presentation?

Why was it better to create a multimedia presentation than a book?

What was the best part of your presentation?

What did you find easy to do?

Did you find anything difficult?

What skills did you use?

What new skills did you learn?

Who was your audience?

If you were doing this task again, what would you do differently?

For some aspects of the work, particularly the ICT skills, you could use a tick sheet (see Figure 8.1). Pupils could also use smiley faces or scales from 1 to 5 or 10 to record how well they think they did (Figure 8.2).

While we can probably get a pretty good idea of what level the pupil is achieving in ICT using this task, by focusing on the learning objectives, the processes involved in achieving them and ongoing, critical evaluation, we can make assessment more productive than simply marking the point the pupil has arrived at.

Skills used to navigate between pages	Can do	Can do with help	Need to learn
Add a transition effect			
Add a sound effect			
Add a button			
Insert a hyperlink			
Make a timed transition			
Have a voice-over when the page opens			

Figure 8.1   An example of a tick sheet for a multimedia presentation activity

In my presentation the balance between images and text is (circle one):

☹   😐   ☺

The audience will understand what the infants did on their trip

1   2   3   4   5

Figure 8.2   An example of a self-evaluation sheet for a multimedia presentation

Summing up

We usually think of assessment as being something we do to measure a child's achievement, but in effective classrooms it is something that is happening all the time. It can be something most school staff do automatically, questioning children to see if they understand what they are being taught, helping them to understand their own learning, and guiding them towards new learning goals. Both aspects of assessment have their place in the classroom. Indeed they are often used together. When pupils are told they have achieved a certain grade they are often also told what it is they need to do to achieve the next level. Assessment then becomes something that is more than just a snapshot of a point in time, but a way of pointing out the way forward.

ICT and literacy

One of the reasons we like computers is because they can make difficult things easier – like writing. They give us perfectly formed, easily legible text every time. They also help us to create beautifully formed sentences, because we can keep reworking the words until we get them just how we want them. And they can even help us to choose the words we need, either through the use of word-banks or text predictors. We can even talk to them and they will scribe whatever we say. Computers can make reading easier too. There are talking books, CDs, and screen readers – software that reads whatever is on screen.

Using a word-processor

The act of writing is a complex one. It involves doing several things at once – choosing the words to use to get the point across and putting these in a pleasing order, remembering how to spell those words and remembering how to correctly form the letters that make them up. And between all these words and the thoughts they convey we have to put punctuation to make it all make sense. With a computer we can do this one bit at a time.

The writing process has four stages:

Planning
Composition
Editing
Publishing

All four can benefit from the use of a computer.

Planning

There are several ways in which we can plan with a computer. We can begin by listing key points and then fleshing them out. Or we can use a writing frame, a structured template with sentence starters. Or we can use brainstorming or mindmapping software (see Figures 9.1 to 9.3).

In these figures, software called Inspiration has been used to get down all the ideas for a piece of discursive writing about school uniform. The links between topics, and the offshoots from each, can be seen clearly, but it doesn't look very structured. However, as with most software of this kind, with one click you can change the diagram into a more structured one.

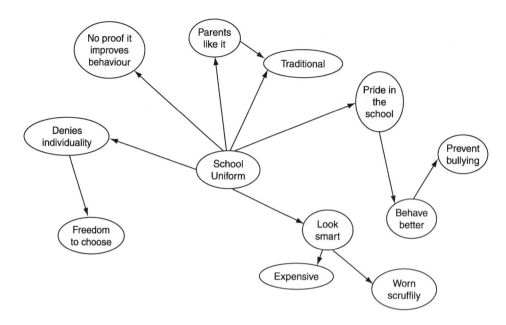

Figure 9.1 A brainstorm about school uniform

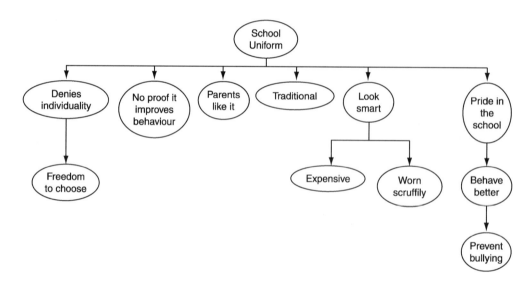

Figure 9.2 Brainstorm about school uniform re-formatted as a structured diagram

And one more click can send it to a different program to begin a piece of work. This could be a presentation, a website or, in this case, an essay.

We can also plan by using a writing frame. There are six styles of non-fiction writing in the National Strategy, each of which has a particular form that can be used as a starting point. Discursive writing might follow the following pattern:

Some people think that . . .

One argument for this is . . .

Another point is . . .

Also

However, other people think . . .

They believe that . . .

Having looked at both points of view, I think. . . .

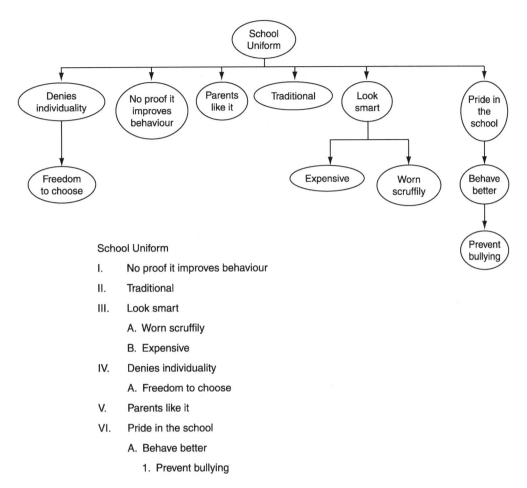

School Uniform

I.   No proof it improves behaviour

II.   Traditional

III. Look smart

     A. Worn scruffily

     B. Expensive

IV. Denies individuality

     A. Freedom to choose

V.   Parents like it

VI. Pride in the school

     A. Behave better

        1. Prevent bullying

Figure 9.3   Brainstorm about school uniform as an outline for writing

It is possible to create templates in a word processing program for sort of this exercise very quickly and easily:

- type in the sentence starters
- choose Save As from the File menu
- give the document a name such as 'Discursive template'
- from the 'Save as type' box, choose Document template.

When you want to use the template, choose 'New' from the File menu. The template you created – with just the sentence starter in it – will appear in the document window. Children can open it, work on it, give it a new name and save it. The original will be preserved for others to work on.

Composition

'Composition' means getting the text down. When composing we needn't worry too much about spelling, grammar and phrasing – we can come back to those. Now we just need words on a screen to work with.

Other aspects of the process can be distracting and so you might want to turn off the squiggly red and green lines that MSWord uses to show where the mistakes are. The red lines are for spelling mistakes, which can lead children into constantly checking, and even then not always getting everything correct. When you are not confident in your own abilities there is a tendency to believe that the machine can do what you can't, so if it suggests a correction it might be accepted, even if it is wrong. For this reason it is often best to turn off the automatic spellchecking and support children to work through it all afterwards, either using the spellchecker, or a dictionary and a printout. As for the green lines, these are for grammar and can range from simply putting in too many spaces to 'fragment, consider revision', whatever that means. To get rid of the wavy lines follow Tools>Options>Spelling and grammar, then uncheck the boxes beside Check spelling as you type, and Check grammar as you type.

When getting their thoughts down some pupils might use some interesting spellings, a lot of which might be good phonetic guesses, while others may seem quite random. It will help to have them read their work out loud in order to understand what it is they want to say. They can even record this and listen back while following the text for themselves.

Editing

Having got the words down, children can now turn to the part in the process where they polish and refine their text to accurately express their ideas. At first they can simply read through and see what mistakes they can pick up. Some word-processors, especially those designed for the classroom, will read work out loud. This is very helpful for identifying missing words and particularly wayward spellings. They can also run the spellchecker and see what suggestions the computer has, but for some children this should be done with support as they may not be able to identify the proper spellings, nor have the confidence to know when they have got it right and the computer is wrong, as can happen with spellings of people's names.

Despite the support of the machine it is always advisable to print out and read a draft because, for some inexplicable reason, we easily miss mistakes on screen that are obvious on paper. No one knows why.

It is a good idea to use a font size of between 12 point and 18 point, as larger fonts are easier to read, and a line-spacing of either 1.5 or double, as wider lines are easier to read and the printouts have more space to make corrections by hand.

Publishing

Every piece of work will have an audience of some sort. This could be the class teacher, when the worked is marked, or the public, when a work such as a poem goes onto a wall display in the school entrance or an account of a trip goes onto a school website. The way in which the work is presented will be determined by how it is going to be seen and the needs of the audience.

A poem on a wall will probably need some visual enhancement: clip art, a background image, a border, different colours or styles of font, will all help to convey its meaning. A web page needs to be presented in short bites of information that are easily taken in by people who don't spend long on a page before moving on. A story in an exercise book needs to be properly laid out, correctly punctuated and written to meet the learning objectives of that lesson.

By breaking the writing process down it becomes much more manageable for all children, with results that often exceed those that would be achieved with just a pencil and paper.

Hints for using a word-processor

The following hints are provided to make writing easier while using a word-processor.

- First, work directly onto the computer, don't spend time copying out handwritten work. The power of the computer is in its capacity to help us form our thoughts by working and reworking them. If we just want a neat copy of what has already been written the time would be better spent practising handwriting. The pupils don't always have to do the typing. As long as it's their words it matters less who is entering them.

- Second, use a clear font. There are lots to choose from these days but very few that follow the conventions of the letters we teach children in handwriting. This can occasionally lead to confusion, with some of the more decorative ones being positively obscure. Most fonts write 'a' as an upside down 'g', of the few that don't 'Comic Sans' and 'Sassoon' are most commonly available.

- Third, spread the work out. Use at least 1.5 spacing. This makes it both easier to read and to edit.

- Fourth, turn off the spelling and grammar checkers so that children can concentrate on getting the words down and not be offered the sometimes welcome distraction of automated accuracy. (See the Composition section above for how to do this.) You might also want to turn off some of the 'Auto correct' features such as the ones that automatically capitalise new lines, very annoying when you are writing a list and you have to keep changing upper case to lower. Follow Tools>Auto correct options then uncheck the relevant boxes. (Incidentally, if you accidentally write in the wrong case, or forget to capitalise the first letters in titles, you can correct this by highlighting the text, holding down the Shift key, then pressing F3 on the very top row of the keyboard. This will toggle through: all capitals; all lower case; and first letter capitalised; on each press of F3.)

- Fifth, do the final editing on a hard copy – you'll be surprised what is missed on screen. You can also check spellings this way so that you can limit the number children focus on to a targeted few, and get a more accurate picture of their abilities than when the computer helps them out.

- Finally, find 'the one who knows'. There are times when just about anyone using a computer gets stuck. It will have done something you just don't understand. Someone, somewhere will know what to do, and it won't necessarily be an adult. Cultivate them.

Aids to writing

Although word-processors in themselves provide much support to the writing process sometimes pupils need a bit more help, particularly if we want them to work independently. There are a range of programs that offer similar sorts of support.

Talking word-processors

As the title suggests, these are programs that read your work back to you as you write. They will do this at letter, word and sentence level, or when a word is clicked, or when a section is highlighted and a toolbar icon clicked. Examples include:

- Talking Write Away
- Write Outloud
- Clicker 5
- Talking First Word
- Softease Studio
- Texthelp Read and Write.

By reading back at letter level they let the child know they have pressed the correct key. However, they usually say the letter name, not the sound, and so are less helpful for developing phonic awareness.

At word level they reinforce spelling, although any phonetically correct word will be read. 'Cow' and 'kow' therefore will sound the same. A couple of programs get round this by also pulling up graphics or symbols. 'Clicker 5' has around 3,000 graphics that will drop into the text, and 'Writing with Symbols' (see below) has a vast array of line drawings representing not just nouns but abstract ideas such as 'love' and 'inside'.

When reading the whole sentence the computer helps children to know if what they have written makes sense and is what they wanted to say.

Word-banks

These are lists of key vocabulary – words, phrases or whole sentences – that can be clicked on to create all or part of the text. Typically these will appear in a box on the screen for children to select from. Examples include:

- Clicker 5
- Writing with Symbols
- Talking First Word
- Softease Studio.

Text predictors

This is increasingly common technology as mobile phones have it available when people are writing text messages. As you begin to write the word the computer tries to guess what it might be and offers a list for you to choose from. As it gets to know your style it will begin to predict even before any keys have been pressed for the next word. This cuts down keystrokes and lets pupils focus on what they want to say rather than having to remember how to spell the whole word. Examples include:

- Co:Writer
- Penfriend
- Texthelp Read and Write.

Speech to text

With this software we can do away with the keyboard all together and simply talk to the computer, which transcribes what we are saying. This technology is now impressively accurate. However, while it might appear to be the answer for pupils who find creating texts difficult, there remains the problem of finding the words you want to get down. Forming thoughts is often part of the problem, and while removing the barriers of spelling and keyboarding can be helpful, it is only part of the answer. The major part of the task remains – knowing what you want to say. Again this is increasingly common technology, with some tablet computers coming already equipped with it. The market software leader is 'Dragon Dictate Naturally Speaking'.

Aids to reading

There are a couple of things we can add to our computers to make life easier for pupils who find reading difficult. But we can start simply by creating exercises on a word-processor.

For a start we can use the 'Highlight' tool to pick out key words in a prepared text. If we use a variety of colours we can create a colour-coded rhyming scheme on a poem. Or examine the grammar of a text by making all the verbs red, the adjectives green and the nouns blue. This is particularly helpful as a group exercise on a whiteboard.

Then we can create reading exercises. A key skill is to be able to read for information. To practice this we can enter a piece of text then ask pupils to delete everything except the information they need. This could be used in history, for instance, to make notes from historical records. An account of an event such as the Great Fire of London can be copied from the internet into a word-processor, then everything except the key incidents deleted, leaving a skeleton of the text with just the important parts remaining.

If you want to use a text repeatedly, either for different purposes or over time, simply save it as a template in the Save As dialogue box (see the Planning section earlier on in the chapter for how to do this), then it will be protected from changes.

Visual help

While 'Writing with Symbols' purports to be about creating texts, it is largely about reading them. By providing a visual cue for every word, pupils get a prop in much the same way as is provided by illustrations in early storybooks. They can look at the picture, work out what's happening and decode the text. Other software, such as 'Clicker 5', will also work with sets of symbols.

Screen readers

Do what they say, read what's on the screen. Very helpful for reviewing work, browsing the internet and finding information from CD-ROMs. They can be set to read what is highlighted or simply to cycle through everything on the screen reading it as they go. 'Texthelp Screenreader' is a good example of this.

Cloze programs

Cloze is where words are missed out of a text and pupils have to fill them in. A good example of this is 'Clozepro', where options are given for how much help pupils are given for completing the text. However, one program that has had a lot of influence in this area since the early days of educational computing is 'Developing Tray', although it is only really a cloze program in a very broad sense.

'Developing Tray' is designed to be used with a group, preferably with a big display such as an interactive whiteboard. A text is put up, but some of it is missing. This can range from all of it to just a handful of key letters. The missing ones are either replaced by a character such as '=', or by nothing at all, which makes it much harder. The aim is to re-write the text. When working collaboratively pupils hear each others' ideas and their strategies for decoding. This gives pupils an insight into how their classmates are thinking, about how they go about reading and understanding texts. A great help for those who are developing literacy skills, as well as a challenge for those for whom these are secure.

Great for group work

As with the 'Developing Tray' example above, computers are great tools for working collaboratively. Even a standard monitor is big enough for a reasonable number of people to gather around and see what is happening. And the provisionality, the capacity for change, means the group can easily debate and discuss what it is they want to say. When we are being creative it is often helpful to be able to bounce ideas off other people, to let them help shape our thoughts.

We can also work together without being in the same room, or even on the same continent. The use of video-conferencing and email means that pupils can share ideas with others who they have never even met. One way of doing this is to work together to write a story. Each child writes a paragraph then sends it on for others to add to, who send it on again and so on, until the story comes back to whoever started it to see how it has turned out.

Computers can open up writing, and reading, for children regardless of their abilities. Everyone will benefit from the support that any word-processor can give to the creative process. And for those who find this difficult the fact that creating a text can be broken down into stages, and that other programs can be brought in for added help, lets them work in ways that pencil and paper just can not.

As for reading, electronic voices can be added to electronic information to tell pupils what it is the text is saying to them. Or we can find ways of analysing texts to help them to better understand what it's all about.

ICT in mathematics

As subjects, mathematics and ICT have a lot in common. Both require good reasoning skills and methodical approaches. While using ICT can be about research, creativity and communication, programming computers to do what we want them to do is about thinking through the steps in a process in a logical way and putting those steps into a series of procedures that the computer can understand. So there are points at which the two subjects meet and times when using technology helps to put across difficult mathematical concepts.

Programming and mathematics

When teaching pupils how to use a programmable floor robot, or turtle, we often start by asking them to draw regular mathematical shapes. In part this is because having understood the principles to create one procedure we can vary it quite easily to draw a whole host of other shapes. However, it also helps pupils to understand ideas such as the angles of a shape always adding up to 360 degrees. They can build a number of regular polygons, varying the number of sides and finding that each internal angle can be calculated by dividing 360 by the number of sides.

To build a square, pupils can use the command 'Repeat 4 [fd 50 rt 90]'. This will build a square with sides of 50 steps. 'Repeat 8 [fd 50 rt 45]' will build an octagon. Once they've done this shape, they can explore a whole number of challenges – looking at similar shapes by repeating the same procedure and extending the length of the sides, working out how to draw more demanding shapes such as a nonagon (nine sides) or heptagon (seven sides) or drawing a circle by taking small steps to show that it is made up of a number of minute turns ('Repeat 360 [fd 1 rt 1]'. To get a smoother line, the child could use decimals and increase the number of repeats).

Logo is a good program to use to introduce pupils to sequences and flowcharts. Some programs have sequences and flowcharts built in; pupils can watch each step and amend the commands as necessary.

Enhancing teaching and learning

There are a number of ways in which ICT can support the teaching of mathematics: by providing tools that the whole class can share on an interactive whiteboard, using games and activities that are specifically designed for learning about mathematics, using ICT for 'drill and practice' type activities (with these, instead of filling pages of exercise books with notes, pupils complete lots of calculations on screen).

Whole-class mathematics and ICT

As interactive whiteboards become increasingly available, multimedia tools become used more and more to explain mathematical concepts to the whole class. Some software titles are written specifically for teaching with whiteboards, others adapt well.

Among the interactive tool boxes supplied with the board are all sorts of features worth exploring. These include graph papers of different sizes, rulers, stopwatches, dice, counters, protractors and number lines. There are even programs that display the size of an angle as the user draws or manipulates a shape. These features can help us easily demonstrate on the big screen the things we want pupils to do individually. For instance, with Softease Draw, as we create a shape the size of the angles appear. As we pick up the edges and move them around, the angles change. We can instantly show a number of things, such as the angles of a regular polygon, and the different types of triangles.

Another feature often included is a function machine. We put a number into the on-screen machine and another number comes out of the other side. The pupils have to work out what the machine did to the first number to create the second. For instance, if we type in 2 and the second number is 4, then the machine might simply have multiplied by 2. So if we type in 3 we would expect the second number to be 6. If instead it is 7, then the machine is not multiplying by 2. It might be multiplying by 3, then subtracting 2. By doing this activity on the whiteboard, or a monitor all the pupils can see, with everyone sharing their ideas, thoughts and strategies, pupils can learn from one another.

It is possible to create a function machine quite easily in Excel. One way is:

- type into one column the various calculations you want the pupils to discover
- 'pull' the sides of the column together so that the calculations are hidden
- copy the answers into another column.

Alternatively, you can put the calculations on a separate worksheet from the inputs and outputs.

Individual mathematics and ICT

Integrated learning systems can also support the development of mathematical skills. These are automated systems in which the computer sets the sums for the pupil to answer. The system adjusts the questions it asks depending upon how well the pupils do. If a child does very well the questions get harder until the child starts to get the answers wrong. If the pupils does less well the questions are easier until the child gets them consistently right. A record is kept of the answers given so that reports can be produced for the class teacher in case they need to use targeted teaching for any areas of particular difficulty.

Other exercises and games can also support mathematical learning, for example, learning about angles by playing billiards or the problem of 'how can you get a fox, a chicken and a bag of corn safely across a river?'. When doing these kinds of activities, it is important that pupils articulate their strategy in some way, either by writing it down or explaining it to someone else. Otherwise, while they might be able to complete the exercise, they might not understand the 'why' or the 'how' of it. The role of the teaching assistant is to ask questions that can help them say what it is they have done.

Mathematical software, activities, games and tools

There are a lot of tools available specifically for teaching mathematics but resources can also be found in some of the more 'open' software titles; you can also use some of these to build your own tools. 'My World' has shape stamps that can be used to build blocks or create tessellations. 'Clicker 5' has screens that can compare the time on digital and analogue clocks. And, although we might use a drawing package for an exercise about planning the layout of a room, drawing the area to scale and creating stamps to represent furniture, we could also do this exercise in MSWord.

Online tools can be used to explore laying out a space, such as a garden or kitchen. The BBC website has a Virtual Garden Tool that can be used for planning a layout. Some of the DIY stores, including MFI and IKEA, have room-planning tools for laying out kitchens and bathrooms.

These kinds of games, activities and tools are important because the learning is valid, that is, it is based in reality. Pupils have to do actual measuring in order to use the virtual tools. The task can be related to the children's immediate experiences and environment, particularly if the redesign actually goes ahead. While the tools are virtual, the activity is practical and provides everyday application for the mathematics.

On-screen tools can also be used to explore patterns and tessellations, such as those found in Islamic art or even the Pop Art of Andy Warhol. Shapes or images can be repeated across a page then changed in a number of ways, including colour and contrast.

Other day-to-day uses of mathematics with computers include converting or transforming data from one form to another, such as when converting from Fahrenheit to Centigrade, miles to kilometres and Sterling to Euros. As with the function machine, one number can be entered into a formula. The computer does the calculation and gives the answer. A spreadsheet formula to convert kilometres into miles would simply be to divide by 8 and multiply by 5. So 40 kilometres would convert like this, '=5(40/8)'. With a less direct conversion such as that with temperature scales the method is to draw a line graph and read across from one to the other.

ICT and mathematical learning

Having pupils use a computer to do complex calculations allows them to focus on results and save time that they might otherwise have to spend on the mundane part of an exercise. A simple example of this is the magic square. The numbers 1 to 9 can be put into a 3x3 square so that each row, column and diagonal equals 15. By using a spreadsheet to try to solve this problem, pupils can use trial and improvement, moving the numbers around and watching the answers change until they get the required result. They don't need to recalculate each line every time.

Using ICT to teach mathematics encompasses more than just using computers. In early years settings, ICT and mathematics might be the toy till and the activity of giving money and receiving change. Further up the school pupils might be exposed to digital readouts, perhaps to compare them with analogue ones such as clock faces, scales and measuring devices. They might use accurate measuring devices such as stopwatches or sensors. And, of course, they might use calculators, some of the first ICT devices to become widely owned and used.

ICT is in many ways integral to mathematics, in the way it shares skills, concepts and processes, and in ubiquitous technology such as calculators. It is of course important that pupils understand the calculations that are necessary to solve a problem. But what ICT tools do is remove the drudgery from the process and let pupils focus on analysing results. Electronic technology can greatly enhance pupils' understanding of complex concepts by means of interactive teaching tools. It has become easier to demonstrate, model and explore what can be very abstract ideas. And ICT supports the practise of skills learnt. The pages of calculations that pupils used to have to write out to make sure a process had been learnt can now be replaced by on-screen questions, targeted to the pupil's individual level and adjusted as the activity progresses.

CHAPTER 11

ICT across the curriculum

It is a requirement in schools that ICT should be used in teaching and learning in every subject. The only exception is PE at Key Stage 1. While that might at first seem like a tall order, it is not difficult to achieve given the breadth of resources and educational experiences that ICT covers.

One obvious way to use ICT is with interactive whiteboards. These will doubtless be on the walls of every classroom in the very near future. Even TVs, CD players, tape-recorders and overhead projectors can be thought of as ICT. The important thing is the context in which they are used. Instances might include:

- listening to a story on a CD player while following the text in a book;
- skipping through a DVD to find a particular piece of information;
- using a digital voice recorder to interview a local historian about the area, then using that recording as part of a walking tour;
- gathering data on the noise from a nearby road using sound sensors for an environmental science project.

In all these instances the ICT is not the focus of the activity but the tool for the job.

The skills to use the tools

As electronic technology becomes more embedded into classroom practice, the ways in which teaching assistants will be expected to support children will need to change. The following is a list of some of the skills and knowledge areas that will be useful for working in ICT-rich educational environments:

- setting up equipment, such as connecting a DVD player to a TV, a printer to a laptop, a video camera to a computer;
- acquiring images from peripheral devices such as scanners and webcams;
- using different sorts of cameras, including digital video, still camera, webcam and Digital Blue;
- filming with a digital video camera and downloading the footage to a computer for editing;
- using webcams or Digital Blues to make stop frame animations;
- taking photos with a digital camera, downloading them onto a computer and doing simple cropping and enhancing;

- managing files, including creating new folders to store work; moving and copying files between folders on a computer; moving and copying files between external sources (CDs, USB keys, cameras) and a computer on a network;
- burning CDs of pupils' work for them to take home, for example, music tracks or animations;
- copying films from the computer back to the camera or to DVD;
- recording sounds on a digital voice recorder and downloading these onto a computer;
- recording sounds on the computer, such as for multimedia presentations;
- searching the internet for pages for pupils to use and bookmarking them;
- copying images and text from the internet to create learning resources;
- finding resources on the internet, such as short films, for teaching purposes;
- sending and receiving emails, with attachments;
- creating electronic resources such as Clicker grids and Powerpoint presentations;
- knowing how to adapt the computer for pupils with special educational needs;
- being aware of developments in new technologies, such as tablet PCs, and the integration of phones, MP3 players and personal digital assistants (PDAs).

While these skills might seem a lot to learn, and feel challenging, you probably already have a lot of them (searching the internet, sending emails). Some aren't particularly difficult (taking photos, burning CDs) and others are very similar (moving files between folders and downloading images from a camera). They are all fairly straightforward; what is important is to approach them with the belief that they are within your reach, simply classroom tools for you and the pupils to use when needed.

You also need to know how to use the different software applications pupils have available to them. While these work in many different ways, they have some common functions, such as opening, saving and exiting.

ICT in different subjects

Below are some of the ways in which ICT can be used to support different curriculum subjects. The resources mentioned under a subject are not necessarily unique to it. What you can do is become confident in using them, so that when a learning opportunity presents itself you can work right across the curriculum.

PE

In PE we can use ICT to both record and analyse performances, and to keep track of results. We can:

- use spreadsheets to analyse results over time, both individual and team performances;
- calculate the nutritional value of our diet, again on a spreadsheet;

- video individuals and teams to see how they are playing and what they could do to perform better, then compare it with how professional sportsmen and women do it;
- use interactive dance mats in lessons.

Science

There are a lot of very good science simulation programs around that show things we couldn't easily see by other means: a beating heart, the germination of a seed, the relative movements of the Sun, Moon and Earth to create day and night, the seasons. There are also ICT simulations we can create ourselves:

- stop-frame animation can demonstrate how a plant grows, how a knee joint works, and the principles of classification;
- short films can show experiments and investigations rather than simply writing them up; a video will show the practicalities of hydraulics better than a written account can;
- heat sensors can test the properties of different types of insulation and show temperatures changing over time;
- time-lapse photography can show a shadow changing in the school playground over the course of a day;
- a webcam can show tadpoles developing in the school fishpond.

History

A lot of the work we do in history is text-based – both reading and writing about events and using images to retell stories – but there are also multimedia resources available. The BBC website has a lot of 3D animations, such as walking across London Bridge in the sixteenth century or entering a trench in the First World War. You can also re-fight historic battles, including Hastings and Waterloo, to see if a different result was possible.

You can also:

- use a desktop publishing package to create front pages for historical events: 'Gunpowder plot discovered', 'King loses his head', 'Queen Victoria "Not Amused" ';
- design an advertising campaign with multimedia presentation software to sell inventions and discoveries of the past – potatoes, the steam engine, electricity;
- make a virtual filmstrip with Kar2ouche of famous events, such as the story of Henry VIII's six wives;
- show film clips of famous points in the twentieth century from the Pathé News archive, such as the first Moon landing or Gandhi's visit to the East End;
- interview older local residents about changes to the area, recording them on a digital voice recorder and using them in a local history presentation.

Geography

Tools available in geography range from recording images and sounds of the local area, to looking at it from above on aerial photographs. You can:

- compare maps of the local area with aerial photos by overlaying one on the other using either maps.google.co.uk or www.multimap.co.uk;
- use Google Earth to share information from a field trip;
- create digital postcards, exchanging information by email with a school in another country to compare your neighbourhood and theirs; send and receive digital photos, and exchange information about the school day, the climate and things that are found in both places, such as hamburgers in a fast-food restaurant.

Religious education

In RE you can use still or video cameras to record visits to local places of worship. There are a number of reference works available that can help with this activity, which may include recording evidence of what people believe. 'Faiths and Celebrations', for example, is a CD that gives straightforward explanations about the beliefs and festivities of the six major religions in England.

Art

ICT is a very visual tool and, as well as taking and manipulating photos, there are all sorts of ways pupils can use it in art. They can:

- try out different styles of work on screen – oil or watercolour for instance – before painting for real;
- explore the styles of famous artists – the repetition of Andy Warhol; the patterns of Bridget Riley; the lines and blocks of colour of Mondrian – through using a drawing package;
- project a photo onto paper stuck to the wall with an overhead projector or visualiser copy it using different techniques;
- create collages by cutting and pasting electronic images;
- scan pupils' paintings and redraw them with different colours, shades and tints.

Citizenship

Throughout their time in primary school, pupils are expected to develop the skills of being active citizens, mainly by learning to communicate effectively – talking and listening, participate in decision making and think about ideas and issues. ICT can support the development of all of these. Pupils can:

- make use of video films to think about body language and gestures, to understand that we communicate with more than just words;
- use tools on the school website to post messages about proposed changes, such as a new playground layout, and to vote anonymously on these;

- search the internet for information for presentations and debates;

- use software to explore different scenarios, such as bullying;

- share ideas and hold debates within and beyond school via email;

- use some of the many websites around to measure the impact on the world of individual pupils, and of the school as a whole, such as www.globalfootprints.org;

- share ideas with brainstorming software on a whiteboard that can then be used to structure debates and discussions.

Design and technology

ICT can be used to research, to design, and to explore simulations. Pupils can:

- use the internet to research different designs of common objects such as chairs;

- draw different nets of packaging to work out which is the most cost effective;

- design the appearance of the packaging;

- use a computer connected knitting machine to produce a wall hanging;

- explore simulations of different sorts of engine;

- create and test electrical circuits with simulation software.

Music

The capacity for ICT to create music is well known, as a lot of what we hear these days has been electronically generated. Pupils can use the mouse and keyboard to 'play' any instrument, given the right software. They can sample and mix, play and record. Not only can they experiment with different sounds, but they can use them to compose their own tunes, and explore the way in which rhythm works.

They can also share their compositions with a real audience, either through the internet by uploading onto a school website, or by creating a podcast, by burning CDs or transferring to MP3 players.

Across the internet there are websites where you can mix different sounds, change pitch, tempo and rhythm, and generally try out tools that were, until recently, confined to the recording studio.

As the use of ICT in schools develops, we find it becoming embedded and no longer notice it is there. Just as we might reach for a pencil and paper to do a particular task we reach for a mouse, camera or handheld computer whenever we need them. ICT gives pupils opportunities to engage in learning in new ways and new fields, to the extent that their experience of school will be quite different to ours and probably to their children's as well.

CHAPTER 12

ICT and inclusion

Computers and all their associated paraphernalia are marvellous tools for inclusion. They both make the curriculum more accessible for pupils who find learning difficult in some way, and also help to make learning a richer, more rewarding experience for everyone.

How we learn and how ICT helps

There has been a lot of interest in recent years in how the brain works and how we learn. This has resulted in two particular theories about learning: learning styles and multiple intelligences.

Learning styles

The learning styles theory is based on the idea that we all learn from seeing, hearing and doing: we are all visual, aural and kinaesthetic, which has become known by the acronym VAK. While we all learn in these three ways (and by smelling and tasting, although there is less focus on these two in schools) it is thought that each of us prefers a particular style. For instance, when learning a foreign language some of us like to see words written down, some like to listen to what is said and some want to combine speech with movement such as gesture.

The VAK approach can be seen when young children are learning phonics. For example, the teacher could give a phoneme an action to match its sound, and so the children might mime a snake slithering along their forearms, as they say 'ess' and the teacher shows them the letter S.

As multimedia tools, computers are very good at presenting information visually and with sound. The kinaesthetic bit is the use of hands to operate a keyboard and mouse, particularly for activities involving moving things around by 'dragging and dropping' or building simulations. Meeting individual pupils' preferred learning styles becomes easier when using a computer.

Multiple intelligences

The multiple intelligences theory has been around for about twenty years. It is a reflection of the thinking that in education we tend to celebrate traditional academic achievement, which some children may not find easy, while ignoring the other kinds of success. Originally there were thought to be seven different intelligences, but this number has grown over the years to nine. In each intelligence, ICT can help to develop and demonstrate pupils' achievement. Here are a few ways it can do this:

- Verbal-Linguistic Intelligence – children express themselves by writing stories on a word-processor.

    They enjoy scripting videos, creating podcasts and interviewing other people by email or video-conference.

- Mathematical-Logical Intelligence – children collect and analyse data, looking for patterns and finding ways of presenting this as graphs and pictograms.

    They enjoy programming floor turtles, and creating procedures in Logo.

- Musical Intelligence – children have a good appreciation of aspects of music such as rhythm and pitch and find it easier to remember things they sing or hear on a soundtrack.

    They enjoy creating and recording their own melodies and songs.

- Visual-Spatial Intelligence – pupils work with images.

    They enjoy taking pictures, videotaping and editing video as well as thinking about layouts of web pages and designing 3D objects to be created by computer controlled machines (CADCAM).

- Bodily-Kinaesthetic Intelligence – pupils move around and make things.

    They enjoy using models, whether making animations or controlling Lego robots as well as acting on DVDs and learning languages through a dance mat.

- Interpersonal Intelligence – pupils are aware of the thoughts and feelings of others, are able to empathise and work collaboratively.

    They enjoy using communication tools and activities such as video and music-making.

- Intrapersonal Intelligence – pupils focus on their own thoughts and feelings, working things out for themselves.

    They enjoy making diaries (including video entries or online blogs) and using tools such as mindmaps to clarify their thinking.

- Naturalist Intelligence – pupils are interested in the natural world.

    They enjoy using cameras, microscopes, and journals, and creating databases of finds that can be searched and categorised.

- Existential Intelligence – pupils think about the big picture.

    They enjoy using the internet to research philosophical questions such as 'Why do we need to use animals in medical research?' and discussing and developing their ideas through communication tools such as emails and bulletin boards.

ICT and special educational needs

New technologies are proving to be great tools for supporting pupils with a range of special educational needs. Apart from desktops and laptops, sometimes equipped with specialist software, there are other useful tools, including:

- CCTV cameras and visualisers for visually impaired pupils to use for reading;
- speaker systems to make it easier for hearing impaired pupils to listen to the teacher;
- handheld spellcheckers for dyslexic students;
- webcams to help pupils with autism rehearse and understand different expressions and emotions;
- Braille pads for blind students to get instant translations of texts;
- communication aids to speak on behalf of pupils who find speaking difficult;
- a portable word-processor for dyspraxic pupils who find it easier to type than to handwrite.

However, the most common device used to support pupils with special educational needs is still a standard computer. There are two main ways we can adapt this to make it more useful: we can change the way it works or we can add something else to it.

Changing how the computer is set up

PCs (computers that use Windows) and Apple Macs both have built-in ways to change the way they look and work for people with special needs. Since most schools use Windows, the examples here are for that operating system, however you can make the same changes with a Macintosh too.

Changing the mouse
About 17 per cent of the population are left-handed and most of these either use the mouse with their right hand or swap it across and click the right hand/left hand buttons accordingly. However, it is easy to change the buttons on the mouse. Follow Start>Settings>Control Panel>Mouse>Change primary and secondary buttons. While you are in the mouse properties dialogue box, you can make the pointer easier to see by changing its style or colour or adding a trail to it. You can also speed up or slow down the click speed or have the pointer jump to an active button in a dialog box.

Changing the keyboard
The keyboard dialog box is also in the control panel. Here you can change the rate at which the cursor blinks and letters get repeated if a key is held down. This is helpful for those who find it difficult to lift their hands. If you open the Accessibility Options dialog box, adaptations to the keyboard include Sticky Keys (the Shift, Ctrl or Alt keys can be operated one press at a time instead of by holding down two keys at once), and Filter Keys (computer doesn't repeat letters if the user doesn't lift their hand quickly enough). You can also switch on Mousekeys, which allow you to control the pointer with the numeric keypad instead of the mouse.

Changing the appearance
Some pupils with visual impairments need the screen to look different, with higher contrast colour combinations or bigger icons. Some pupils with dyslexia might find it easier to work with colour combinations such as red and pink, or

blue and white. In the Accessibility Options dialog box the Display tab lets you change to a high contrast one, usually either white on a black background, or vice versa. The look of the screen can also be changed through the Display Properties dialog box. Under the Appearance tab there are options for changing not only the colour of the desktop but also, if you click the Advanced button, the colour used for the background and fonts of the active Window. In other words, you can change how any application looks to one the pupil finds easier to work with.

Wizards

While it is easy enough to use the Control Panels, there are also built-in features – wizards – that make the changes for you. If you follow

    Start>Programs>Accessories>Accessibility>Accessibility Wizard

a number of dialog boxes pop up that ask questions about how well you can see the screen, hear the sounds or use the keyboard. These will let you make many of the changes listed above quite straightforwardly. Also in the same area are tools such as the Magnifier, to enlarge sections of the screen, the on-screen keyboard, and the Narrator, which will speak letters as they are typed and actions as they happen.

Adding to what you've got

If you cannot get the computer to work in a way that best supports your pupils, you probably need to add something else to it. This could either be hardware, or software, or both.

Adding hardware

The main ways that we control the computer are through the mouse and the keyboard, although we might also use the monitor or give the computer verbal commands.

The mouse

The most common alternative to a mouse is a joystick. Lots of home computers already have them connected for playing games with. Those for pupils with physical impairments tend to be designed differently, without the buttons to fire ray guns or accelerate cars. They will have a left and a right button, as with a mouse, but the movements are controlled by the stick itself. There will usually also be a 'latching key', which is pressed to take the place of holding down the left mouse button. Those who use electric wheelchairs often prefer a joystick as it works in much the same way as they drive their chair.

Trackerballs are also quite common. This is like turning the mouse upside down so the ball is at the top, the device stays still and the fingers move the ball. Again these will have similar button configurations to a joystick. You may well have used one of these when using a public internet connection.

Some trackerballs are designed to work with small movements and slip easily onto a finger to be controlled by the thumb. Another device for those with limited movements is a touchpad, just like on a laptop only attached via a cable so it can be moved to a convenient position.

One of the most widely used technologies for people with physical impairments are switches. These often take the form of buttons that the user presses to move the cursor and to make selections. These can be placed anywhere the pupil has sufficient movement to control them, so while they will commonly be within reach of their hands they might also be mounted for use with a foot, the head or an elbow. As well as single presses, some work through being squeezed or knocked from side to side. They can even be operated by breath with a 'sip and puff' system, which is what Stephen Hawking uses, even to the extent of writing his books.

A stylus can also replace the mouse. This is used with a special drawing pad or the screen itself, as with a tablet PC.

The monitor

The tablet PC is a different sort of monitor. We can interact with it directly, without a mouse or keyboard. Similarly, we can interact directly with a touch screen. As the name suggests, control is gained by using your finger on the screen. You might have come across this hardware already, in public places such as automated ticket machines at railway stations.

Voice control

Voice control is not strictly a hardware adaptation, but it is a different way to control the computer and requires a microphone headset for giving commands and receiving feedback. The idea is that you simply talk to your computer and it does what it is told to do. This technology is not new, as it has been around for about 20 years, but it is beginning to be built into computer operating systems. What has changed is the amount of training the user (and computer) now need. This has lessened and now every aspect of operations, from switching on to closing down, can be controlled with spoken commands.

Specialist software

There are all sorts of programs that can meet the needs of individual children, especially in the area of literacy (see Chapter 9). These programs can support pupils by:

- reading work back to them through 'text to speech';
- providing word-banks;
- predicting what the pupil is trying to say;
- adding symbols or graphics to text to make it easier to read;
- taking dictation.

Software for pupils with special educational needs

Some programs are designed to meet very specific needs, while others can be used more generally. The capacity to enlarge what's on the screen for pupils with visual impairments has already been mentioned. Not only are tools built into Windows but they can be added on, such as 'Zoomtext', which offers more options.

For pupils with physical impairments there are programs that are designed to work with a mouse that has been altered, or switches. Instead of clicking, the user lets the pointer dwell on a word, letter or command to select it. This is one option with 'The Grid', which can be used as a communication aid, and a writing tool. Another way to use it is entirely with switches, either one or two, depending on how much capacity the user has to control them. The selector function can advance automatically, or the user can move it forward by clicking with one switch, then the chosen word is selected by a click on the other switch.

Pupils with autistic spectrum disorders need to be taught to recognise and understand emotions and expressions and how, why and when people show them. Emotions and expressions can be explored with the program 'Smart Alex' but a more sophisticated one is 'Mind Reading', a library of over a hundred video clips of actors demonstrating different feelings.

These pupils can also benefit from rehearsing new situations. 'Karzouche' is a program that helps them create 'social stories', and think about what may arise in a new context and work through how to behave.

Subtitles are now widely used for people who are deaf or hearing impaired. There is a limited range of interactive stories available to use on computers that include signing. However, this may change as work continues on 'eSIGN', a project supported by RNID, to provide instantaneous, signed translations of materials, including web pages with computer-generated avatars. In the not-too-distant future deaf people may be less dependent on human translators to sign for them.

Finally there are programs that can help pupils with social, emotional and behaviour difficulties. 'EBD' is a term that encompasses a wide range of problems, from being overly introverted to continually disruptive. There are a number of things we can do here: one is to monitor challenging behaviour to identify when and where the issue is worst. We can do this with any database program such as 'Excel'.

Another thing we can do is help pupils think about and reflect on their behaviour. A good tool for this is 'Ways Forward', which has been designed following the principles of solution-focused brief therapy, which, as the term suggests, looks for ways to move on rather than dwell on the past.

Another way to help is by using 'Bubble Dialog' (which can be downloaded for free from the internet). The program takes the form of a two-sided conversation, with associated speech bubbles, for pupils to explore difficult situations. The idea is that often when we say one thing we may actually be thinking another; for instance, when someone is picking a fight it could be because they are worried about the comments of their peers if they back down.

ICT can be used to provide curriculum tasks and activities that challenge and extend gifted and talented pupils. It can help them work to a higher level than they otherwise might. For instance, when accessing information on the internet they might 'go beyond' books that can be found in the school library to read academic treatises. They might access an 'expert's' site, where they can ask questions that school staff might find difficult to answer. The NASA site features many different kinds of scientists, such as astronomers, physicists and geologists. To find them, visit www.nasa.gov and type 'ask a scientist' in the search box.

You can take a similar approach with Google. Just search on 'ask an expert'. The problem will be finding the expert you want and knowing who is worth using. The www.howstuffworks.com site has hundreds of articles on just about anything, ranging from earthquakes and computer viruses, to dreams and déjà vu.

You can also guide pupils to use the more advanced elements of computer software, for example, creating procedures in 'Logo' that ask for different variables before they run or using multiple layers in photo editing software. There may be times when the children's abilities with the ICT resources begin to outstrip the staff's. This is one of the great things about ICT, that teachers and learners can swap places, as we can all learn something new from someone else.

As technology advances, gifted and talented pupils may become the 'early adopters' – people who embrace the latest tools first. An example of advanced software is 'Mission Maker', which can be used to create authentic computer games. The program provides richly textured 3D environments but the challenge is to create an experience within the environment that feels like an authentic game, making events inter-dependent and using elements such as objects to collect, time, and energy levels.

Supporting pupils for whom English is an additional language

Pupils acquiring the English language can benefit in several ways from using ICT. There is the potential to present information in multiple formats, speech and image, with software such as 'Writing with Symbols' (whose intended audience is actually pupils with learning and literacy difficulties).

ICT is also intensely patient, so activities can be repeated endlessly and identically as pupils learn the particular nuances of English pronunciation. Just using a voice recorder can help them, by having them listen and repeat words and phrases, and listen to themselves say it back. You do the same activity in MSWord by using the Insert sound facility (usually in Insert>Object>Wave Sound; it varies from version to version).

Another helpful tool is web-based translation. From the front page of Google a click on 'Language Tools' gives access to instant translations to and from English and at least nine other languages. For a second opinion you could visit www.altavista.com and use their 'Babelfish' tool, which includes translations between languages other than English, such as from Portuguese to French. These tools have limited use as the languages are mostly those of the wealthier rather than emerging nations (so Bengali, Somali and Serbo-Croat are not to be found). A search for online dictionaries in almost any language should provide some help.

ICT opens up possibilities for supporting all pupils, particularly those whose learning needs warrant additional attention. Not only can we adapt the computer and add to it, we can modify the tasks we want the pupils to do. This can mean offering more support or making more demands and setting bigger challenges. Because of the multimedia presentational possibilities and the activities now available the curriculum is becoming deeper and more enriched by new technology, creating engaging and motivating learning experiences for all pupils regardless of their needs and abilities.

Appendix

The National Curriculum Attainment Targets

Level 1
Pupils explore information from various sources, showing they know that information exists in different forms. They use ICT to work with text, images and sound to help them share their ideas. They recognise that many everyday devices respond to signals and instructions. They make choices when using such devices to produce different outcomes. They talk about their use of ICT.

Level 2
Pupils use ICT to organise and classify information and to present their findings. They enter, save and retrieve work. They use ICT to help them generate, amend and record their work and share their ideas in different forms, including text, tables, images and sound. They plan and give instructions to make things happen and describe the effects. They use ICT to explore what happens in real and imaginary situations. They talk about their experiences of ICT both inside and outside school.

Level 3
Pupils use ICT to save information and to find and use appropriate stored information, following straightforward lines of enquiry. They use ICT to generate, develop, organise and present their work. They share and exchange their ideas with others. They use sequences of instructions to control devices and achieve specific outcomes. They make appropriate choices when using ICT-based models or simulations to help them find things out and solve problems. They describe their use of ICT and its use outside school.

Level 4
Pupils understand the need for care in framing questions when collecting, finding and interrogating information. They interpret their findings, question plausibility and recognise that poor quality information leads to unreliable results. They add to, amend and combine different forms of information from a variety of sources. They use ICT to present information in different forms and show they are aware of the intended audience and the need for quality in their presentations. They exchange information and ideas with others in a variety of ways, including using email. They use ICT systems to control events in a

predetermined manner and to sense physical data. They use ICT-based models and simulations to explore patterns and relationships, and make predictions about the consequences of their decisions. They compare their use of ICT with other methods and with its use outside school.

Level 5

Pupils select the information they need for different purposes, check its accuracy and organise it in a form suitable for processing. They use ICT to structure, refine and present information in different forms and styles for specific purposes and audiences. They exchange information and ideas with others in a variety of ways, including using email. They create sequences of instructions to control events, and understand the need to be precise when framing and sequencing instructions. They understand how ICT devices with sensors can be used to monitor and measure external events. They explore the effects of changing the variables in an ICT-based model. They discuss their knowledge and experience of using ICT and their observations of its use outside school. They assess the use of ICT in their work and are able to reflect critically in order to make improvements in subsequent work.

Resources and software

Information about the curriculum in schools

www.becta.org.uk
Government agency responsible for ICT in schools in England.

www.nc.uk.net
The National Curriculum Online.

www.ncaction.org.uk
Advice on implementing the National Curriculum and examples of children's work.

www.qca.org.uk
The Qualifications and Curriculum Authority, responsible for devising the National Curriculum.

www.standards.dfes.gov.uk/schemes2/it
The ICT scheme of work online.

Sources of information on the internet

www.ajkids.co.uk
Ask Jeeves for kids – a search engine specifically for children.

www.altavista.co.uk
A search engine, but also has 'Babelfish' an online translation tool.

www.bbc.co.uk
One of the best websites there is, an endless source of information and activities.

www.britishpathe.com
Home of Pathe News, whose films you may be able to download and use in lessons.

www.cia.gov
Home of the CIA Worldbook for up-to-date information about every country in the world.

www.dictionary.com
An online dictionary.

www.globalfootprints.org
A site devoted to showing how much of an impact we make on the planet.

www.google.co.uk
The most-used search engine in the world. Its name has entered the language.

www.howstuffworks.com
Covers just about anything you could want to know about.

www.maps.google.co.uk
Interactive maps, including aerial photos and overlays.

www.multimap.com
Well-known website for providing maps.

www.nasa.gov
Full of information, including photos of distant planets.

http://safety.ngfl.gov.uk
Advice on internet safety for children.

www.wikipedia.org
An online encyclopaedia that anyone can contribute to.

www.yahooligans.com
A search engine for children.

Software references

2Email
www.2simple.com

Bubble Dialog
www.dialogbox.org.uk

Clicker 5
www.cricksoft.com

Clozepro
www.cricksoft.com

Co:Writer
www.donjohnston.com

Decisions3
www.blackcatsoftware.com

Developing Tray
www.2simple.com

Digital Blue
www.taglearning.com

Dragon Dictate Naturally Speaking
www.dyslexic.com

eSIGN
www.rnid.org.uk

Faiths and celebrations
www.sherston.com

Inspiration
www.taglearning.com

Kar2ouche
www.immersiveeducation.com

Logo
www.blackcatsoftware.com

Mind Reading
www.jkp.com

Mission Maker
www.immersiveeducation.com

Mswlogo (free download of Logo)
www.softronix.com/logo

Penfriend
www.dyslexic.com

Smart Alex
www.inclusive.co.uk

Softease Studio/Softease Draw
www.softease.com

Talking First Word
www.rm.com

Talking Write Away
www.blackcatsoftware.com

Texthelp Read and Write/Texhelp Screenreader
www.dyslexic.com

The Grid
www.sensorysoftware.com

Ways Forward
www.waysforward.net

Write Outloud
www.donjohnston.com

Writing with Symbols
www.widgit.com

Zoomtext
www.aisquared.com

Glossary

Here are just a few of the words and abbreviations you will come across when talking about ICT. There are several good glossaries and dictionaries on the internet and in the bookshops if you need them.

AAC	Augmentative and assistive technology – additional tools for people with special needs, particularly communication difficulties.
Absolute Cell reference	Part of a spreadsheet formula that doesn't change when copied to other cells.
ADSL	A fast connection to the internet – broadband.
application	Software.
assistive technology	Additional tools for people with special needs.
attachment	A document sent with an email that is not part of the message itself.
back up	Make a copy of computer files in case something goes wrong.
bit	Smallest unit that computer files are measured in.
bitmap	Type of graphic file where each point on the screen is logged, like a cross between a graph and painting by numbers.
bookmark	Keep a note of a web page so you can return to it.
Boolean search	Type of search using operators such as '+' or 'AND', '-' or 'NOT' to filter results.
boot	Start up a computer.
broadband	Fast internet connection.
browser	Software used to access the internet.
bug	Problem with a computer's software.
byte	Larger unit of measurement for computer files.

CAD/CAM	Computer aided design/computer aided manufacture – planning a product on a computer then linking to a machine to create it.
case sensitive	Reacts to upper and lower case letters.
cell	Box on a spreadsheet.
compatibility	Able to link up to other parts of the computer, both hardware and software.
concept keyboard	Flat pad that can control the computer through touch.
cookie	Instructions from a website to a computer that can track use.
CPU	Central Processing Unit – the bit of the computer that does the working out.
CSV	Comma Separated Variables – standard format for moving information between databases.
data	Collection of information.
database	Means of managing a collection of information.
dial up	Connecting to the internet over an ordinary telephone line.
digital	Generally something captured in an electronic format such as music or a photo.
Digital Blue	Pupil-friendly video camera with associated software.
domain name	The name and location in a website address.
download	To copy something from one place to another, usually from the internet.
dpi	Dots per inch, the means of setting the quality of a printout.
drag and drop	Method of moving text and images around.
FAQ	Frequently Asked Questions. Usually found on websites.
field	Space each piece of data is entered into.
file	Anything created and saved on a computer.
file extension	The three or four letters after the file's name that tells the computer what program to use to open it.
firewall	Means of preventing hostile attack on a computer from outside.

Flash	Program often used for games and animations, especially on the internet.
folder	Place where a collection of files is stored.
font	The type style, the design of the lettering.
formula	A calculation on a spreadsheet.
free text	A field in a database without restrictions on the type or amount of information that can be entered.
FTP	File Transfer Protocol – a way of getting pages onto the internet.
GIF	Type of image file.
gigabyte	Big unit of measure of computer space.
graphics	Images.
graphics card	Part of the computer that puts the images on screen.
GUI	Graphical User Interface – what you see on the screen that you can click on to operate the computer.
hard drive (or disk)	The permanent memory store in the computer, as opposed to a floppy disk that can be removed.
hardware	The parts of a computer that you can feel.
Home page	Opening page of a website.
HTML	Hyper Text Mark Up Language – the programming code web pages are written in.
hyperlink	Text or image you can click on that takes you to somewhere else.
icon	Image on screen that represents something, an action or a company for instance.
input device	Means of getting information into the computer, such as a keyboard or microphone.
ISDN	A fast connection to the internet.
ISP	Internet Service Provider – a company that connects users to the internet.
Java	Programming language used on the internet for games and animations.
JPEG	Type of image file.
LAN	Local Area Network – group of computers linked together that are in one place.

megabyte	Large unit of measurement for computer files.
MIDI	Hardware that links a computer to a synthesiser.
MLE	Managed Learning Environment – software that sets and marks students' work and gives out reports.
modem	Hardware to dial up to the internet.
monitor	The screen.
MPEG	Type of movie file.
multimedia	Bringing text, sound and images together in one creation.
netiquette	Rules of behaviour for internet users, such as, 'don't use capital letters' because it is the equivalent of 'shouting'.
Network	Group of computers that are linked together.
Newsgroup	Web-based group with a common interest who exchange information.
notebook	Type of laptop.
OCR	Optical Character Reader – means of automatically entering information from a written page.
online	Connected to the internet.
palmtop	Computer that can be held in the hand.
PC	Computer that uses the Microsoft operating system.
PDA	Personal digital assistant – a sort of palmtop.
PDF	Portable Document Format – standard format for documents shared on the internet.
peripheral	Hardware attached to a computer, such as a scanner or printer.
POP 3	Type of email account.
port	Where you link extra devices to the computer.
Predictor	Literacy software that suggests the next word the user will want.
program	Software.
QWERTY	Standard keyboard – these being the first six keys of top line of letters.
RAM	Random Access Memory – the working memory on the computer.

ROM	Read Only Memory – information that can't be changed.
Router	On a network, the hardware that decides which route information will take.
RTF	Rich Text Format – standard format for sharing text files.
search	A way of interrogating information on a database, or of finding it on the internet.
search engine	Web page that helps you find what you are looking for.
search term	The words you use to look things up.
sensor	Device for inputting information such as temperature.
software	The workings of a computer that you can't touch.
sound card	Part of the computer that handles sound.
speech engine	Software that makes the computer talk.
switch	A means for people with special needs to control a computer.
terabyte	Biggest unit yet of measuring computer capacity.
touch screen	Screen that controls the computer through a touch-sensitive surface.
tracker ball	Alternative to a mouse where the user rolls a ball directly with their hand.
Trojan	Type of virus that sneaks up on the computer.
upload	To add files, usually to the internet.
URL	Uniform Resource Locator – address of a website.
USB	Universal Serial Bus – standard way of connecting peripherals.
VDU	Visual Display Unit.
virus	Program that attacks the computer.
visualiser	A cross between an overhead projector and a CCTV camera for throwing up large images for everyone to see.
VLE	Virtual Learning Environment – computer-based learning system.
VR	Virtual Reality – on-screen depictions of actual or pretend 3D situations.

WAN	Wide Area Network – computers linked together over a broad geographical area.
wild card	Used in searches to broaden the terms. For instance 'W*' would bring up all entries beginning with 'W'.
wizard	Part of software that helps you to do a job.
worksheet	Working area of a spreadsheet.
write protect	Stop information on a disc from being over written.
WYSIWYG	What you see is what you get – when you print something it looks like the screen.
zip	Way of making files smaller so they are easier to move around.

Index